"He who has once used deception will deceive again."

—ROMAN PROVERB

SECRETS *from* GRANDMA'S ATTIC

SECRETS *from* GRANDMA'S ATTIC

A SHADOWY PAST

DeAnna Julie Dodson

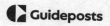

Guideposts

Secrets from Grandma's Attic is a trademark of Guideposts.

Published by Guideposts Books & Inspirational Media
100 Reserve Road, Suite E200
Danbury, CT 06810
Guideposts.org

Scripture references are from the following sources: *The Holy Bible, King James Version* (KJV). *The Holy Bible, New International Version* (NIV). Copyright ©1973, 1978, 1984, 2011 by Biblica, Inc. Used by permission of Zondervan. All rights reserved worldwide. www.zondervan.com

Cover and interior design by Müllerhaus
Cover illustration by Greg Copeland at Illustration Online LLC.
Typeset by Aptara, Inc.

ISBN 978-1-959634-28-7 (hardcover)
ISBN 978-1-959634-20-1 (epub)
ISBN 978-1-959634-29-4 (epdf)

Printed and bound in the United States of America
10 9 8 7 6 5 4 3 2 1

A SHADOWY PAST

Chapter One

I hope I'm not interrupting anything." Amy Allen stepped inside the familiar entryway of the old Victorian house that had once belonged to her grandmother. "I had a few minutes to kill, so I thought I'd see what you're up to."

Her sister, Tracy Doyle, smiled and shook her head as they went up the stairs to her office. "Not at all. I was taking a coffee break. Want some?"

"No, thanks." Amy took a seat next to Tracy's desk. "I'm about coffeed out for now. You remember my neighbor, Deb? She invited me over for a chat a little while ago."

"That sounds nice." Tracy sat behind her desk. "Where are the kids?"

"They're playing with Miles's two while I run some errands." Amy glanced at her watch. "I'm supposed to pick them up at four, so I still have a little time."

"So Jana and Matt are playing with Natalie and Colton again," Tracy said with an insinuating look that only Amy would pick up on.

"Jana and Natalie are in second grade together, and Matt and Colton are both in sixth. Why shouldn't they be friends?"

"No reason," Tracy said with a touch of a smile. "But I remember when you used to date their dad. I thought you were pretty serious back then."

"We were, but everything's different now, and Miles and I are only friends."

"Nothing wrong with being friends," Tracy said lightly. "Or more than friends."

Amy rolled her eyes. "You're so subtle."

"Okay, so I won't be subtle. Are those old feelings coming back now?"

"Maybe," Amy admitted. "Maybe they never really went away."

Tracy laughed.

"What about you?" Amy asked. "Are you sure you don't mind being here all by yourself over the holiday?"

"It's not like it's Christmas or anything. It's just Labor Day."

"But your family usually does something special over the long weekend."

"True," Tracy said, "and my family *is* doing something special. Jeff and Chad went camping, and you know I always support father-son activities. And while Chad's out of town, Anna took their kids to see her family before the baby comes. And then Sara and Kevin took their kids on a trip to the beach. So that covers my husband and my son, my son's family, and my daughter and her family."

"But it doesn't cover you," Amy protested.

Tracy gestured to the stack of books, papers, and folders covering her desk. "This is my something special." She grinned. "Do you know how hard it is to get a little quiet writing time around here?"

"Yes," Amy said, a smile touching her lips. "I have a couple of kids too, you know, and mine are still at home. But you're a reporter. You write all the time with your family around."

"Yes, but most of the time it's like juggling torches. It's nice to have a little peace and quiet to get some of this done before I'm fighting off a deadline again."

"What is all this?" Amy took a closer look at the chaos on her sister's desk and frowned at the slick pages of the book that sat open there. "Isn't that your yearbook?"

"It is. I've been trying to think of a good human-interest piece for a while now, and I came across it when I was looking for a pair of shoes in the bottom of my closet. I flipped through it and realized several of our old classmates have had interesting things happen to them since we graduated. I could get a good story out of that, don't you think?"

"You mean like a 'where are they now?' kind of piece?"

Tracy nodded, a spark of excitement in her eyes. "What do you think?"

"Not bad. Not bad at all." Amy looked over the open page with its photograph of a smiling girl with perfect teeth, perfect hair, and a perfect complexion. "I remember Tommie Hiller, cheerleader, student council, honor society. Are you going to write about her?"

"Nah," Tracy said. "From what I can find, there's nothing really interesting about her post-graduation life. Low-level corporate management. But look here." She turned a few pages. "Dave Winston? He owns a huge tech company in Silicon Valley."

"You're kidding." Amy squinted at the picture of a heavyset boy whose uncertain smile showed the glint of braces. "It's always the quiet ones."

"And then there were the Hernandez twins, who stopped that robbery in New York City. Tony's been in a wheelchair ever since, but he and Mike got law degrees, and they do advocacy work for crime victims."

"I heard about that robbery, but I didn't know what they did afterward. That would make for an exciting story."

"Then there's Bryan Ulmer."

Amy thought for a moment. "Did I know him?"

"He was in the Twin Towers on 9/11."

"Oh, yeah," Amy said soberly. "I did hear about that. That's sad."

"And it's almost the anniversary of that day again. I can't believe it's been so long."

"It was terrible."

"I always felt bad for Bryan. He always said he would make it big, and he never did. He was only thirty-two."

"He was the one who was nearly killed in that car wreck when we were in school, wasn't he?"

"Yeah," Tracy said. "He took his dad's car without permission and ended up flipping it. Nobody thought he'd make it. He had to have surgery to repair his skull and everything. I think it was pretty touch-and-go for a while, but then he returned to school like nothing ever happened. Except for some pretty gruesome surgery scars, I mean."

"I definitely remember that. I didn't know him, but I heard about him."

"I remember him telling one of the guys in my class that he figured since that accident didn't kill him and his dad didn't kill him for wrecking the car, he'd probably live forever. He was sixteen then."

Amy sighed. "And half his life was already over."

"I haven't done much research for my story yet, but I did find out he was an investment broker in New York before he died. He was about to be indicted for fraud when 9/11 happened."

"Why'd you have him sign your book? I didn't think you two were actually friends."

"He just came up and signed it and told me his autograph would be worth a million bucks someday. He never suffered from self-doubt."

"His story is kind of sad though. I don't think you should end your piece with him."

"Definitely not. I'll pick one of the more upbeat ones for the end. Like Chris Marks. He's a big Broadway producer now."

"Oh, right. He's the one you had a crush on when you were in theater, wasn't he?"

"Okay, yes, he was very cute. He was also totally not interested in me or anything else that would get in the way of his theatrical career."

"Hey, that reminds me." Amy pulled the book toward herself and turned several pages. "What about Eve Sendry? Oh, wait, that isn't her real name, is it?"

"No, it's Kitty McAllen. Why?"

"She's in town right now."

"Is she? How do you know that?"

"I saw a poster at the bakery. She's doing a dinner theater on a riverboat in town."

"Oh, she'd be perfect." Tracy found a pencil and a piece of scrap paper. "Do you remember the name of the boat?"

"Um, something to do with luck," Amy said. "*Lucky Chance*? I think that's it."

Tracy thought for a minute. "I'd really like to go out there and see if Kitty—I mean Eve—would give me an interview. Do you have time to come along?"

Amy checked her watch again. "I'd like to. I'm sure it would be interesting to hear what she's been up to all this time. Let me call Miles and see if it's okay for the kids to stay with him a little longer than we'd planned. I don't think it'll be a problem."

A few minutes later, Amy and Tracy parked at the dock where the *Lucky Chance* was tied up.

It was a grand-looking boat, gleaming white, with a big paddle wheel in back and twin smokestacks on top of its double decks. It must have been wonderful to sail down the Mississippi on it, taking in all the sights from the upper deck. Amy could imagine gentlemen in tailcoats and brocade vests and ladies wearing picture-frame hats and hoop skirts and carrying parasols, all waving from the rails.

She stopped to look over the old-fashioned signboard that announced Eve Sendry in the dinner theater production of the mystery *Night of Terror*.

"That sounds fun," Tracy said as they boarded the boat.

"The poster I saw made it look like something set in the 1920s or '30s," Amy told her.

"Dinner too. Maybe Jeff and I will come see it when he gets back from his trip."

"Don't wait too long," Amy advised. "I think they're only here a week or so before they head for another stop down the river. Probably won't even be in Missouri for long."

"Then we'd better—"

"Sorry, ma'am."

Amy and Tracy stopped at the bass voice.

"We're not open to the public yet," the stocky man said, settling the box he carried more firmly against his shoulder. "You'll have to come back when the ticket office opens at five thirty or call the number on the sign to make reservations."

Tracy put up her hand, shielding her eyes from the sun behind him. "We're not here to get tickets. I'm an old friend of Eve Sendry, and I was hoping she'd have a minute to see me."

"I'll go check," the man said. "Who do I say wants to see her?"

"I'm Tracy Doyle, but she knew me as Tracy Allen. And she'll remember my sister Amy too."

"I'll tell her. You'll have to stay right here, understand?"

"Sure," Tracy said.

"Thanks," Amy added, almost certain that this was as far as they were going to get today.

To her surprise, less than a minute later, a tall, slender woman wearing a silver silk robe and with her auburn hair in curlers hurried onto the deck, arms outstretched.

"Tracy Allen, so good to see you!" She pulled Tracy into a hug and then threw her arms around Amy, her blue eyes sparkling. "Amy. Oh, both of you, I'd know you anywhere. I was afraid nobody I knew would still be living in Canton. It's been so long. Come inside, come inside."

"We hope you don't mind us dropping in on you," Tracy said. "I know you have a performance tonight, but I just found out you were in town, and I was hoping to do an article on you for my paper."

"You're a reporter?" Eve asked.

"For the *Lewis County Times*. I want to do an article on what's happened to some of my graduating class. Who better than the world-famous Eve Sendry? Or should I call you Kitty?"

"Eve would probably be best," she said. "I haven't been Kitty in at least thirty years."

"Eve, then," Tracy said. "Do you have time?"

"Oh yes," Eve said. "I'm supposed to be napping, but I was just lying in my bed being bored. I don't really have to start getting ready for a couple of hours yet. You and Amy come this way."

Amy followed them into what looked like a theater lobby and then down a long, plush-carpeted hallway to the left, past several closed doors, until Eve finally stopped at one and threw it open.

"My quarters are a little small, since boats don't generally have a lot of extra space," she explained, "but they're cozy."

Lavender was obviously her favorite color, judging by everything from the rug to the drapes to the cushions on the couch, and the room did look very comfortable. She offered Amy and Tracy places on a love seat upholstered in cream with narrow purple stripes and then sat down in the off-white damask wingback chair across from them.

"You even have lavender roses," Amy said, admiring the vaseful on the coffee table.

"Aren't they lovely?" Eve said. "They're from an investor who wants to become a partner in the show. He's much too flattering. Look."

She picked up a card from the table and handed it to Amy, and Tracy leaned over Amy's shoulder to get a look at it. *To Eve, whose charm and talent assure us of artistic and financial success now and into the future. Rudy.* The letters were bold and confident, rather spiky, and rather distinctive. This Rudy was definitely a take-charge type of person.

"How exciting for you," Tracy said. "It looks like all your hard work might finally be paying off."

"He's awfully optimistic about the show," Eve said. "Now, tell me what you want to know." Then she waved both hands. "No, no, tell me what you've both been up to all these years."

Amy managed to hide a smile as Tracy told Eve about her husband, children, and grandchildren. Kitty, or Eve now, Amy reminded herself, had always been dramatic and excitable, and it had surprised exactly no one when she went into acting.

"So I work from home and at the paper," Tracy said, finishing up. "I have a desk at the *Times* and an office upstairs in my grandmother's old house."

"I remember that house," Eve said. "A Victorian beauty, and of course it's great to work from home when you can."

"I love that part especially," Tracy said.

"What about you, Amy?" Eve asked. "Husband? Children? Fabulous career?"

Amy chuckled. "No husband, not yet, anyway, but I have two adopted children, Matt who's eleven, and Jana, who's seven. And, yes, I have a fabulous career. I'm a first-grade teacher."

"Oh, good for you," Eve said. "That's so important. You must have the patience of a saint."

"I enjoy it, but what about you? It sounds like you lead a very exciting life."

"I love it," Eve said. "Ever since I took drama in high school. Oh, look." She went to her bookshelf, rummaged around a little bit, finally pulled out her yearbook, and flipped to a page toward the back. "There I am in *The Importance of Being Earnest*. And there you are, Tracy. Oh, how young we were."

The two of them discussed teachers and classmates from back then and the fun they'd had.

"What about your family, Eve?" Tracy asked, taking out a notepad and a pen. "Do you mind if I take notes for my story?"

"Not at all," Eve said. "And I'm sorry to say there's not much to tell. My husband died a few years after we divorced, but we did have a son together, Flynn. He's supposed to meet me here tomorrow. He lives in Kirksville, so this is as close as I get when I'm working. We always try to get together when we can."

"That's wonderful," Tracy said as she took notes. "I've always been glad my kids and grandkids live nearby."

"But tell us about the play," Amy urged. "The sign says *Night of Terror*. It's a mystery, right?"

Eve's eyes lit up. "It is. Sort of an Agatha Christie cozy-type thing. Very 1930s, very British, snappy dialog, and all that. I get to put on my posh accent," she said, changing her voice to match her words. "You should both come."

Amy looked at her sister. "I think it would be fun."

"I'd love to," Tracy said. "I've wanted to see you in something ever since I heard you became an actress."

Eve put her hand on Tracy's arm. "Who would ever have thought it when the two of us were in Mrs. Schaefer's drama class?"

"Well, I knew I was never going to make it to Hollywood, but I think everybody was sure you would."

Eve gave her a rueful smile. "The only thing I ever got in Hollywood was a couple of parts in B-list movies and a no-good husband. But, honestly, live theater is so much more fun." She tossed back her head and lifted one shoulder, a diva's pose. "And where else would little Kitty McAllen get to be the star and not just a walk-on?"

"I'm sure you're amazing," Tracy assured her.

"I'll do," Eve said, clearly pleased. "But it is a fun show, and the dinner is delicious. The only thing I wish is that Lyle would spend more on some of the props."

"Lyle?" Amy asked.

"Lyle Pinson. He owns the *Lucky Chance* and puts on the shows. He's been known to pinch a penny till it begs for mercy."

"I'm sure putting on a play, especially a historical piece, is expensive," Tracy said.

"True, but we do a pretty good business too. I think he takes in a lot more than he admits to, but I guess that's none of my business. He pays me what I'm due, and I can't really complain. Still, ugh. There's a folding screen we have in the play, you know, one of those tall ones that could be used for a room divider or something?"

Amy nodded, knowing exactly the type of screen she meant.

"Well," Eve continued, "the one we have is the most awful-looking thing. I mean, it could have been bought at one of those everything-for-a-dollar-type stores. It's not nearly nice enough to be displayed in Lady Frances's drawing room."

Tracy and Amy both laughed.

"Maybe you could just leave it out of the scene," Amy suggested.

"That wouldn't work," Eve said. "Lady Frances's cousin has to be kidnapped from behind it. It's vital to the plot."

"Oh." Amy thought for a moment. "Tracy, what about that screen Grandma Pearl had up in the attic? It seems like that would work."

"I think it would." Tracy turned to Eve. "Our grandmother had one, dark wood with beautiful carving and mother-of-pearl inlays. If you promise nothing would happen to it, I think we could lend it to you. How long would you need it?"

Eve clasped her beautifully manicured hands together. "Would you really? That would be wonderful. We're doing *Night of Terror* until we get down to the gulf. We're changing to *The Girl in the Beaded Dress* once we head upriver again, and we won't need the screen for that. I could return it to you when we're back in Canton a few weeks from now. Would that be all right?"

"That would be perfect," Tracy said. "And maybe by the time you do *Night of Terror* again, your boss will spring for better props."

"Good luck with that, but I guess there's always a chance." Eve smiled. "But now you'll have to come to the show. My treat. It's the very least I can do to thank you."

"All right," Tracy said. "We'd love to, wouldn't we, Amy?"

Amy nodded. "We sure would."

"Are you free Sunday night?" Eve asked, her forehead slightly puckered. "I know we're sold out tonight and tomorrow, but I think there are a few seats left for Sunday. I'll have to check for you."

"That should be fine," Amy said. "We can bring the screen over sometime tomorrow if it's okay, and then you can let us know about the tickets."

"I can definitely do that," Eve said. "You two don't know how happy I am to have that screen. It's so much easier to act, I mean really act, when the setting is right."

"I'm sure." Tracy picked up her pen again. "Now what about my interview?"

It didn't take long for her to get enough information for her story. True, Eve Sendry's movie career was less than stellar, but she had won a few minor roles in some Broadway productions when she was in her twenties and thirties. Even now, in her midfifties, she made a good living traveling around doing the live productions she loved. It didn't seem like a bad life, cheesy props and all.

Amy pulled out her phone as soon as she and Tracy left Eve's cabin.

"I'd better call Miles and tell him I'll be over to get the kids."

"It was nice of him to let them stay a little later than you planned," Tracy said.

"Yes, it was."

"And I'm glad all the kids get along so well. It's almost like they're brothers and sisters."

Amy stopped in the middle of the hallway. "You're really subtle, you know?"

Tracy smirked. "I didn't say anything. But you know—"

She broke off at the sound of angry voices coming from behind a door bearing a brass plaque that said LYLE PINSON OFFICE.

The two sisters looked at each other and then stepped back into the arch of a closed doorway.

"I don't want to get tangled up in somebody's fistfight," Amy whispered.

Tracy nodded. "Let's wait a second and make sure it doesn't spill out into the hall."

One of the voices spoke again. It was a man's voice, too low to make out, but the answering one was clear enough.

"And I'm going to prove it!"

Amy frowned. She was almost certain she had heard that second voice before, but she couldn't quite place it. She looked questioningly at Tracy, who gave her a puzzled shrug in return.

The sudden bang of the office door against the wall made them both jump, and neither of them moved as an elderly man came out into the hallway. He was tall and thin, as weathered looking as an old sailor should be.

"I'll prove it!" the man shouted, his face red and scowling, and then he turned to stalk toward the lobby.

Amy and Tracy exchanged another glance. They had both known Robert West for many years. Before he retired, he was the captain of a ferryboat that had carried countless passengers back and forth across the Mississippi River, and Amy had seen him around Canton as long as she could remember. He had always been friendly, quick to share a smile and a story about life on the docks. Amy had never seen him looking so angry. Judging by the astonishment on her face, Tracy hadn't either.

Before they could move, the office door slammed shut again, and the only sound was the lap of the water against the side of the boat and the faint voices of the men working on deck.

Tracy exhaled. "Well."

"Yeah," Amy said, glancing at the office door and then toward the lobby. "That sounded serious."

"I wonder what's going on."

"I know you're a reporter, but I'm sure it's none of our business." Amy took her sister's arm. "Come on. You already have a story to work on."

"Still, nice Captain Robert? I can't imagine what they were arguing about. Maybe Kitty, I mean Eve, knows something."

"You can ask her tomorrow." Amy urged her into the lobby and out into the bright September sunshine.

On the drive back to Tracy's house, neither of them said anything more about Robert West, but Amy was sure Tracy was going to ask Eve about the incident and the old sailor. She was sure too that her sister would get some information on the mystery man in the office while she was at it. And Amy wouldn't mind being there to hear Eve's answers.

Chapter Two

*M*om, can we learn to cook?"

Amy glanced in her rearview mirror to see the reflection of her little girl's earnest brown eyes. "Well, sure you can. Do you want to learn too, Matt?"

Matt's grin was a little more mischievous than usual, but he nodded eagerly. "Could we? And could Colton and Natalie come help? Dr. Miles hasn't really had time to teach them, and he's pretty busy, so they don't want to bother him."

"I think that'd be a lot of fun for everybody," Amy said, her eyes on the road again. "And it's always good to learn life skills. What do you want to cook?"

"Well, Colton says meat loaf," Matt said. "'Cause I told him yours is the best and you could teach it to us."

"And Natalie and him think their daddy would like it too," Jana added.

Amy didn't miss the glare Matt gave his sister.

"I mean," Jana said quickly, "in case they want to make it for him sometime."

Amy smiled. She and Miles Anderson had been sweethearts in high school, but for some insane reason, she had decided after graduation that she wanted more than little Canton, Missouri, and a steady, dependable—not to mention good-looking—guy like Miles. By the time she came to her senses, Miles had moved on.

In the years since then, Miles had become a doctor, gotten married, had children, and gotten divorced. He had only recently come back to Canton, and her kids and his were in the same classes at school and had become best friends. Amy had admitted to herself for a while now that she still had feelings for him, deep feelings, but she feared it was too late to rekindle the spark. It was a shame too, because he was such a nice guy.

"So can we?" Jana pressed.

Amy glanced at her again, nudged out of her musings. "Make dinner with Natalie and Colton? Sure. Do you know what you want besides meat loaf?"

"Mac and cheese!" Jana crowed.

"Yeah, mac and cheese," Matt said. "I already know how to make that. I've done it before."

Amy couldn't help wondering how many times these children were left to fend for themselves before she had become their foster mom and then adopted them for good.

"You can teach Jana and the others how to do it then," Amy told him. "How would that be?"

"Yeah," Matt said, "I can do that. We should probably make a cake or something too."

"Okay," Amy said. "What kind?"

"Pineapple upside-down cake," Jana said without hesitation.

"Pineapple upside-down cake?" Amy said. "Where did you hear of that?"

Jana glanced over at her brother, eyes wide.

"It was on TV," Matt said quickly. "It looked really good."

"Yeah," Jana said. "It was on TV."

Well, they were up to something, that was for sure. But if it was just to get to spend more time with their friends and make a mess in the kitchen, that was all right. They were only kids once.

"Are you sure it's okay with Dr. Miles if Colton and Natalie come over and cook?" Amy asked.

"We didn't exactly talk to him about it yet," Matt said. "We wanted to see if you'd let us first, and then maybe you could invite Colton and Natalie to come so their dad would know it was already okay with you."

"I appreciate that," Amy said. "And, yes, I can call him and see if they can come over. When do you want to do this?"

"Can we do it next Saturday?" Matt asked. "It'd be fun to do it tomorrow, but the guys are playing softball, and I told them I'd come."

Amy's eyes met his in the mirror. "You were going to tell me about that eventually, weren't you?"

"Yeah, uh, I kinda forgot, but I would have. But can we do it next week?"

"If it's all right with Dr. Miles, it's okay with me, and you two can start out learning about meal planning and make a list of what you're going to need."

"That sounds fun," Jana said. "We'll do it really good."

Amy smiled. They were great kids, and she was glad they were hers.

No matter what they were up to.

Two men waited on the dock when Amy and Tracy returned to the *Lucky Chance* the next day.

"Ms. Sendry said for us to take the screen over to the stage for you," one of them said. He was the stocky man who had told Eve the day before that they wanted to see her.

"Thank you," Tracy said.

"I'm glad we don't have to wrangle that up to the deck and then onto the stage ourselves," Amy said as she and Tracy followed the men onto the boat.

"Always nice to have help," Tracy said. "I hope they'll be careful with it."

"You could always tell Eve you changed your mind."

"Nah. It was only gathering dust up in the attic." Tracy looked longingly at the freshly polished screen as the sailors set it down and leaned it, still folded, against the back wall of the stage. "But it does look nice now that it's all cleaned up, doesn't it?"

"It's gorgeous!" Eve hurried up to the stage, her hands clasped against her heart and her eyes shining. "Oh, it's just perfect, isn't it, Danny?"

There were three men with her, including a young man who looked like Eve. The one she had called Danny looked the screen up and down as if he was calculating to the penny what it was worth.

"That's nice," he said, running his finger across a piece of inlaid mother-of-pearl. "Just make sure your friends know this loan is something between you and them. The show and the boat aren't taking any responsibility, okay, Eve?"

Eve rolled her eyes. "Yes, we all understand. Tracy, Amy, this is Danny Vee, our stage manager. He runs the show and, when Lyle is away, the boat."

"Ladies." He gave the visitors a half-apologetic smile and offered Tracy his hand. "We're glad to have it, I'm sure, but you understand, don't you?"

"Of course." Tracy shook his hand. "I'm Tracy Doyle, and this is my sister, Amy Allen. We went to school with Eve here in Canton."

"Ah," Danny said.

Eve took one of the other men by the arm, a bearded man with graying dark hair and gray eyes, taller and leaner than the stage manager.

"Amy and Tracy, this is Rudy Daheim, the theatrical financier I told you about," Eve said. "Tracy was in drama class with me in high school."

"So you're an actress," Rudy said as he clasped Tracy's hand.

"Not much of one, I'm afraid," Tracy said. "I'm a newspaper reporter."

"Oh yes," Eve said. "She's doing an article about the interesting things that happened to some of our classmates after graduation. Isn't that fun? She's already interviewed me."

"That sounds like a good read," Rudy said. "Successes and scandals, eh?"

"I suppose there could be some scandal in there," Tracy said, "but I haven't found much along that line, at least nothing recent. The one actually shady thing I did dig up is about somebody long dead, so I don't think anybody will be upset over it. It's mostly about people like Eve who came from Canton and have gone on to live interesting lives."

Rudy's mouth turned up on one side. "Now you have me curious about this shady character you uncovered. Someone from your high school class?"

"Yes," Tracy said. "I was going through my yearbook, and I thought his story would make an interesting read. Then I noticed several other people I remembered and decided I'd include some of them in the article too. It was fun to compare their interests and accomplishments at that age to what they went on to do later in life. Some of the things they wrote in my yearbook ended up being very telling. I might even include photos of their comments in my article."

"That does sound interesting," Rudy said, but the remark seemed more out of politeness than actual interest. "I guess I'll have to wait until your article is published to find out the juicy details, am I right?"

"I hope it'll be out in our next edition this coming Wednesday. Or maybe the following Wednesday. We'll see."

"Charming," Rudy said. "No doubt your readers will enjoy it. I'm sure they'd be interested in hearing more about *Night of Terror* too."

"Are you involved with any productions we would have heard of?" Tracy asked.

"Most likely not," Rudy said. "The big boys back the more famous productions. I usually stay in the background, working with smaller investors, giving them an opportunity to have at least a little part of something that brings happiness to a lot of people."

"That's so nice," Amy said. "You must travel around a lot, talking to people and seeing regional productions."

"I do," Rudy said. "I meet all kinds of people all over the country and find a lot of performers who deserve a chance to make it big.

I used to work in an office in New York City, but I can't imagine ever going back to that. I got to where I couldn't stand being cooped up, doing the same thing all the time. Now every day's a new adventure."

"And we're so excited to have him here," Eve said, gazing up at him. "As I told you, he might be investing in the production company."

Rudy smiled. "I'm only having a look at this point, but I'm impressed with what I've seen so far."

"We're excited to see the show," Amy said. "And Eve says it's been sold out, so that has to be a good thing."

"It certainly is," Rudy said. "I think my investors will be interested. In fact, I'm considering putting out a whole fleet of showboats up and down the river. The right properties, the right personnel..." He looked at Eve and Danny. "You just never know."

"It's terribly exciting," Eve gushed. "And we'll be in on it from the start."

"Nothing's settled yet, Mom," the young man said quietly.

Eve patted his arm. "I know, I know. You've probably already guessed," she said, turning to Amy and Tracy, "but this is my son, Flynn Carson."

"Hi, Flynn," Amy said, seeing in his tall, slim build and high cheekbones a definite resemblance between him and his mother.

"It's nice to meet you," Tracy added.

"You too," he said. "Mom said you were helping her out by lending the show that screen. If I'd known, I would have been happy to go pick it up for her."

"That's okay," Tracy said. "We wanted to come back here anyway. Your mom said she would try to get us tickets for tomorrow night."

"I did get them," Eve said. "I put them under your name at will call, but I have a huge favor to ask now."

She glanced at Danny, and he urged her on with a nod.

She turned to Amy. "You remember what a good actress Tracy was in school."

"I always thought so," Amy said, not surprised by Tracy's humble shrug.

"You were always too modest," Eve said to Tracy. "You were delightful playing Helena in *A Midsummer Night's Dream* our senior year."

"But you stole the show as Titania, Queen of the Fairies," Tracy said.

"And I'm sure the play needed both of you in order to be a success," Rudy said diplomatically.

Tracy looked warily at him and then at Eve. "And what does this have to do with the huge favor you want to ask?"

Eve shrugged. "You remember how it was in school. We always hoped and prayed that nobody would get sick or break a leg or anything before opening night because our understudies, if we even had them, weren't all that great."

Amy fought a smile, sure she knew where this was going.

"Somebody broke a leg?" Tracy asked.

"Flu," Eve said, her expression tragic. "Fran is our bookkeeper, but she's filling in a small part for another actress who quit to go to Hollywood last month."

Tracy frowned. "And you didn't hire anybody else in all that time?"

"We did," Danny said, "but she's finishing up a booking in St. Louis. She's due in on Monday. We're dark Monday night anyway, so we thought we'd made it through okay. Then Fran got sick."

Eve grasped Tracy's hand. "She'll probably be okay to go on again by Tuesday, if our new actress doesn't get here. We're just talking about Sunday night."

"What about tonight?" Tracy asked. "You don't have all that much time before curtain."

"We found someone for tonight. Jean, our wardrobe girl. But she's leaving for her sister's destination wedding in the morning. She's had it planned for almost two years, and she says she'll quit if she has to, but she's the maid of honor and she's going to that wedding."

Amy chuckled. "I don't blame her."

"You don't know anyone else who could fill in?" Tracy asked. "Someone from a high-school theater department or something?"

"It's Labor Day weekend," Danny said. "The schools are out, and we've been coming up short in the last-minute fill-in department. We were talking about not even having the show tomorrow."

"We can't do that." Eve looked pleadingly at Tracy. "You know the first rule of the theater business. 'The show must go on.'"

Tracy looked at her incredulously. "You're not asking me to step in."

"Oh, but I am."

Chapter Three

I already told you, it's a small part. It's just the teensiest, weensiest little part," Eve said. "Not even ten lines."

"Why not just cut the role for this performance if it's that small?" Tracy asked.

"Because it's tremendously important. As I said, Lady Frances's cousin—Muriel—is vital to the play. She overhears the villain's plans, is kidnapped because of it, and everything else hinges on that. The rest is Lady Frances and her pretentious niece figuring what happened and why."

Amy couldn't hide a smile. "It sounds perfect for you, Tracy. All you have to do is learn a few lines and some blocking and then take a bow at the end."

Tracy gave her a look that said she knew exactly how much Amy enjoyed watching her try to wriggle out of this, but there was something in her expression that also said she was intrigued by the idea.

"You know I haven't been on a stage since high school," Tracy said. "What about my costume? What about makeup?"

Eve beamed. "We'd take care of all that, wouldn't we, Danny?"

Danny snorted. "Yeah, sure. We can do that. Just don't let Lyle know about it. He'd have a fit if he knew about all the shenanigans going on here while he's gone."

Eve bit her lip and turned to Rudy. "I suppose we shouldn't be talking about all of this in front of you. It doesn't make us look like a very good investment, does it?"

Rudy chuckled. "I've been around theater a good many years. I've seen some of the scrambling that goes on behind the scenes, even on Broadway. I'm actually impressed. This is a good indication that you're resilient enough to handle anything that comes your way." He glanced at the gleaming Rolex on his wrist. "But I'll let you all sort this out. I have another appointment to keep."

"Of course," Eve said. "I hope we haven't kept you too long."

"Not at all. But I do have some potential investors coming to see the show tomorrow night, so I'm relying on you—and you, Tracy— to give us a fabulous performance."

Amy smiled mischievously. "And you can send her some lavender roses too."

Rudy chuckled. "So you saw Eve's."

"That was a nice card you sent with them," Tracy said. "No wonder she's so excited about you investing in the *Lucky Chance*."

Rudy's eyebrows went up. "You showed them the card too? That was very naughty of you, Eve." He shook his finger at her. "Now everyone in the cast will expect to be showered with gifts."

"Of course we will," Tracy teased. "But even without roses, I'm in."

Eve threw her arms around Tracy with a girlish squeal. "Oh, wonderful! Wonderful!"

Rudy smiled. "See you all tomorrow night then."

"I think I'm just in the way here with all this theater business," Flynn said as Rudy walked away. "I'm going back to your cabin, Mom. We still have some things to talk about."

Eve smiled tightly. "All right. I'll be there as soon as I can."

"Are you sure your boss is going to be okay with me stepping in?" Tracy asked Eve once he was gone.

"Lyle?" Eve waved her hand. "He left this morning for Vegas and won't be back till Monday night. By then our new Cousin Muriel will be here, and he won't know the difference."

Danny scratched his stubbly jaw. "Um, you know I won't be able to pay you, Tracy. Not without Lyle knowing you're in the play. And if he finds out, Eve and I both might end up in the river."

"I can pay you, Tracy," Eve said. "It'll just be unofficial. It's not exactly a high-paying gig."

"Of course you won't pay me," Tracy said. "I'm happy to help you out. Just don't expect anything Oscar worthy from my performance."

Eve hugged her again.

"Do you think Lyle would actually be mad?" Amy asked.

"Not that mad," Eve said, sounding a little uncertain.

"But everybody in the company will know," Tracy protested.

Danny shrugged. "They know better than to say anything to Lyle. And as long as it works out all right, there's no reason to tell him, is there?"

"I don't know…," Tracy said.

"Oh, come on," Amy said. "You know you want to. And I want you to."

"I just don't want anyone to be upset," Tracy said. "And what are you going to do with my ticket if I don't need it?"

Amy thought for a moment. "I'd ask Miles, but he's taking his kids to a family party in Ewing. I'll get Robin. I'm sure she'll come. I know she'd love to see your big acting debut."

Robin Davisson was their cousin who owned an antique shop in town. She was always up for something fun.

Tracy was quiet for a moment, and then she smiled. "You're right. It will be fun. Amy, since you're so set on my doing this, you're going to have to help me. Will we be able to rehearse sometime, Eve?"

Eve nodded. "It's just a few lines, most of them delivered from a wingback chair. So you won't have to remember much stage direction, and then you just need a really great scream. You can still scream, can't you?"

There was a wicked gleam in Tracy's eye. "Just try me."

Eve's warm laugh filled the stage. "I knew I could count on you. Danny, would you make a copy of Muriel's lines for Tracy?"

Danny nodded. "All right. I hope you're a lightning study, Tracy."

"I can't promise anything now," Tracy said, "but I used to be."

"It won't be hard," Eve said. "Want to go over it all right now?"

Tracy glanced at Amy with a question in her eyes.

"I don't mind," Amy said, really looking around the stage for the first time. Judging by the chairs and dark wood furniture, this had to be Lady Frances's drawing room. "And, yes, I'll be happy to take notes on the blocking and then help you memorize your lines like I used to when we were in school."

"Maybe whoever is doing the part tonight can help us too," Tracy said.

Eve shook her head. "She agreed to do the part as long as everybody left her alone during the day so she could get ready for her trip. I think we're on our own."

Danny rolled his eyes. "I'm going to copy those script pages for you and get Calvin out here while we still have time. He's the one who kidnaps you, Tracy."

"What about your son, Eve?" Amy asked. "Isn't he waiting for you?"

Eve waved her hand dismissively. "He'll be all right for a few minutes. The young are so impatient."

"He looked like he had something important to talk to you about," Tracy said. "I hate to interfere."

"No, no, it's fine." Eve shook her head. "He wants to talk about finances, and that sort of thing always bores me to tears. I've been trying to put it off for the past couple of days."

"You're the boss," Tracy said finally. "Let's get started."

While Danny went to get a copy of the script and the fictional kidnapper, Eve showed Tracy the blocking for her two scenes. It really was very simple. Cousin Muriel was an elderly woman who did much more listening than talking. All Tracy had to do for both scenes was totter into the drawing room and sit down.

In the first scene, she had only three lines and then had to look startled when she overheard a sinister conversation from behind the screen. In the second, she had six lines where she told Lady Frances and her niece that she was worried about what she had overheard. Then she had to go behind the screen to prove to them that, from her chair, she could indeed have heard the sinister conversation. After that, all she had to do was give the audience a bloodcurdling scream, struggle noisily with Calvin, who would be there waiting for her, and then get off stage through the door behind the screen.

Danny soon came back with papers in hand and a slim, dark-haired young man in tow.

"This is Calvin Dupree," Danny said. "Calvin plays Dennison, the footman. He'll be kidnapping you."

Calvin grinned and shook Tracy's hand. "Nice to meet you. Thanks for bailing us out at the last minute."

"I'm happy to do it," Tracy told him. "I suppose you're taken away by the police at the end of the show."

Calvin shook his head. "Actually, the butler who convinces me to be his accomplice murders me right after I kidnap you. It's all very tragic."

Tracy grinned. "Agatha would be proud."

The young man laughed. "No honor among thieves, I'm afraid."

"When do I come back?" Tracy asked, flipping through the pages Danny had handed her.

"Not till curtain call," Eve said. "I'm afraid Cousin Muriel doesn't make it either."

Tracy grinned. "Good. I think this is all I can handle if I'm going to go on tomorrow night. Will we have time for a dress rehearsal tomorrow?"

"We can do that," Eve said. "Curtain goes up at eight. Guests are seated for dinner at seven thirty. We're all supposed to be in wardrobe by six thirty. Make sure you're here before then. We'll get you dressed and made up, and then we should have time to run through your scenes with everybody else in place, don't you think, Danny?"

Danny didn't look too pleased. "I guess that's better than making everybody show up earlier than usual. But you'll have to make sure the stage is clear before they start bringing the audience in."

"We'll be fine," Eve told him.

"I can come earlier if I need to," Tracy offered.

"But then we wouldn't have everybody else to rehearse with," Eve said. "And it's not like we'll be running through the whole play. Just your two scenes. Are you ready to try them now?"

They did a couple of walk-throughs of both scenes. Amy was pleased to see Tracy fall back into acting so easily. It really was a very small role, but the whole mystery hinged on Cousin Muriel. And even though she only had a small amount of preparation, it was obvious that Tracy was going to do a bang-up job.

"The screen is going to be perfect," Tracy said as Amy drove back to Tracy's house after the rehearsal was over.

Amy nodded. "I think so too. I saw the one they were using. It's not quite the discount-store horror Eve described, but Grandma Pearl's is certainly more convincing. It looks beautiful with the rest of the set. Although if this Rudy guy gets some big-time backers for the show, they ought to be able to buy something nice for themselves instead of borrowing ours."

"He'd sure be a godsend for a production like theirs." Tracy thought for a moment. "I keep thinking I've seen him before. There's something about him that reminds me of someone."

"Maybe online or on TV?"

"Could be. His name isn't familiar at all, but there's something about him. Oh well, it'll come to me at some point."

Amy glanced at her. "Are you nervous about tomorrow?"

"Not much, surprisingly enough. I didn't feel like I was as rusty as I thought I would be."

"You did great," Amy assured her. "If you'd like, you can come have dinner with me and the kids, and we can go over your lines a few more times."

"That would be great. When Jeff's gone, I don't cook much. I know we all usually have dinner together on Sundays after church, but—"

"But you should come over to my place tomorrow too," Amy said. "You shouldn't have to go to a lot of trouble if your own family isn't going to be around."

"I love doing it, but you're right. It doesn't seem quite the same without everybody here."

"Come over, and we'll throw something together for us and the kids. It'll still be fun. And then Robin and I will have our fancy meal tomorrow night during the play."

"Did you invite her yet?" Tracy asked. "It's kind of short notice, isn't it?"

Amy shook her head. "I'll call her when I get home. I still have to make sure the kids have somebody to look after them."

"There is that."

"Olivia, our usual sitter, is out of town for the weekend, but I told you about Deb Patterson, who lives two doors down from us. Her son is in Matt's class, and they play together a lot. I've had Russ over a few times when Deb and her husband wanted to go out, so maybe the kids can go over to her house tomorrow night."

"So you've got at least two calls you need to make right away," Tracy said.

"I guess I didn't realize how many ripples I caused when I pushed you into that play."

Tracy chuckled. "Serves you right. Every last ripple."

"You know you're loving acting again."

"I am. And I'll certainly have a story to tell Jeff when he gets home."

"He's going to be sorry he missed the play," Amy said she pulled into Tracy's driveway. "Anyway, I'll call Robin and Deb and see if they're available tomorrow night."

"Okay," Tracy said. "And I just remembered I have a cake mix in my pantry. Do you want me to throw it in the oven and bring it with me tonight?"

"I think Matt and Jana would love it, but can they help you make the cake? They've been asking me to teach them and Miles's kids to cook."

"That sounds like a lot of fun for everybody."

Amy nodded. "We're scheduled for next Saturday. I think they'll really enjoy it."

"All right. Well, they can certainly help with the cake tonight."

"Perfect. I'll see you at my house as soon as I pick up Matt and Jana."

Tracy went into her house, and Amy immediately called Robin. Once Amy convinced her that Tracy really was suddenly and unexpectedly going to act in a dinner theater production, Robin was thrilled to go too. Deb Patterson was her usual accommodating self and said it was no problem for Jana and Matt to spend the following evening with Russ.

Once that was taken care of, Amy drove over to Miles's house to get the kids. It was a little disappointing that she didn't get to say much more than hello to Miles, but Matt and Jana were in a hurry to get home.

Next time, she promised herself. She'd definitely talk to Miles next time.

"This is so exciting," Robin said as she and Amy hurried onto the *Lucky Chance* the next evening. "How crazy is it that we're going to see Tracy in this show?"

"I know. I'm glad she's just as fast at learning lines as she was when we were in school." Amy glanced around the deck. "It looks so different at night with the lights strung all along the rails and shining in the water and with the wind in the trees and the sound of the river rushing by. More mysterious than it was during the day."

"Perfect for a play called *Night of Terror*, isn't it?"

Amy chuckled. "Definitely."

They followed three couples to the box office and picked up their tickets. Then they followed a tuxedoed usher into the theater. It also looked different than it had in the daytime. The lights were low, just bright enough for the guests to make their way to their tables. The usher seated them and told them their waiter would be right with them.

"How pretty," Robin said, touching the linen tablecloth.

"Very 1930s," Amy said. "The silverware and dishes are perfect. Art deco. And so is this." She picked up the crystal bud vase from the center of the table and smelled the fresh rose it held. "This room sure didn't look like this when Tracy and I were here yesterday. No wonder they sell out most of the time."

"It's very nice," Robin said. "I don't suppose we'll see Tracy until she's on stage."

"I wouldn't think so." Amy glanced at her watch. "That won't be much longer now."

There were small printed menus on their plates, announcing what would be served before each act. After their waiter took their orders and then brought them their crabmeat cocktails, the house lights went down a little more, leaving only the lines of tiny lights that lit the narrow walkways between tables.

The curtain went up, and a young couple in period costume came out and sang some songs from the 1930s. It was a creative way to establish the time period of the play that was about to begin.

After they walked offstage, arm in arm, the lights went up a little. The waiter brought out the *penne della nonna*, and soon Act One began. Even though Amy already knew the basic plot, it was enthralling to see it performed with lights and music and actors in makeup and costumes.

Eve had always dominated the stage in high school productions, and it was clear she hadn't lost that ability more than thirty-five years later. She shone as no-nonsense Lady Frances Lavery and definitely knew how to add a touch of light humor to her role.

By the time the first act was over and the lights went up again, Robin was bursting with theories about who had taken Lord Melbry's priceless coin collection.

"I can't tell you anything," Amy said as the waiter set poached salmon hollandaise with fingerling potatoes and spinach soufflé in front of them. "I'm not going to spoil any of it for you."

"I don't want spoilers," Robin insisted, "but can't you tell me if I'm on the right track?"

"Nope." Amy tasted the soufflé and closed her eyes. "Oh, this is divine."

Robin took a bite of her own soufflé. "Wow. That's amazing. I didn't know it would be this good. But where's Tracy? They've mentioned the cousin a couple of times, but we haven't seen her."

"She's in the next act. Just wait and see."

Once more the lights dimmed, and at last frail Cousin Muriel tottered onto the stage and sank into the wingback chair next to Grandma Pearl's folding screen. If Amy hadn't known better, she would have sworn that Muriel was played by a woman in her eighties. Tracy put just the right amount of warble in her voice and unsteadiness in her step and added a touch of feistiness on top of it all.

In the last scene of Act Two, Cousin Muriel, again seated in the wingback chair, told a dubious Lady Frances what she had overheard in the previous scene. "I tell you, they were behind this screen," Tracy said in her Cousin Muriel voice. "They came in that side door, and I'm sure they didn't know I was sitting here. I couldn't recognize their voices, but as soon as I heard what they said, I realized who stole the coins."

"But how could you tell?" Eve's Lady Frances demanded. "I don't think you could hear them properly from here."

"Pshaw." Tracy pushed herself up with the help of a swan-headed walking cane. "You sit in the chair, and I'll show you."

Eve huffed and sank into the chair. Amy couldn't help smiling to herself as the footman slipped out of the room, unseen by the ladies in the drawing room.

"Now," Tracy said, "I'll go back here, and you'll see." She went behind the screen. "Now I'm going to whisper, and you tell me what—"

There was the sound of a struggle, and Tracy screamed.

"Cousin Muriel!" Eve leaped to her feet, and the stage went dark.

As the audience applauded, the house lights went up again and waiters appeared with a choice of frozen custard, mille-feuille, or chocolate lava cake for dessert. Amy and Robin both chose the mille-feuille.

"That was exciting," Robin said. "Tracy's scream really startled me."

"She did get a little carried away." Amy took a bite of her pastry, a light-as-air raspberry-and-almond creation, and let it melt on her tongue. "I don't know if an elderly lady would scream that way, but it was certainly riveting. They're going to be sorry they only get her for one night."

"True." Robin sighed and took a bite of her own dessert. "And I'm already sorry that she's not in any other scenes."

Amy grinned. "At least you'll finally find out whodunnit."

All too soon, the mystery was solved, Lord Melbry's coins were saved, and his avaricious son, the Honorable Ronald Carstairs, was brought to justice. Lady Frances warned her disappointed niece that she should never be fooled by wealth, position, and a handsome face, and the curtain fell to ringing laughter and crashing applause.

A moment later, the bit parts came out for the curtain call, but when the supporting players came on and those who played secondary parts, Tracy wasn't with them.

"They couldn't want her to come on with the stars, could they?" Robin whispered to Amy.

Amy shook her head, baffled, watching as Lady Frances's niece, Lord Melbry, the Honorable Ronald, and the bumbling police detective all took their bows, followed by Lady Frances herself. No Tracy.

"Do you think they didn't let Tracy take a bow because she's not officially a member of the troupe?" Robin asked.

"I wouldn't think so." Amy frowned. "Maybe she went to change after her last scene and isn't through yet."

"Maybe."

Amy thought for a moment. They had gone over the curtain call yesterday when she helped Tracy go through her lines and blocking. Maybe they'd changed it in their dress rehearsal earlier.

The waiters brought out Roquefort cheese and toasted crackers along with coffee and after-dinner mints while the cast members mingled and socialized with the guests. Eve made a beeline for Amy's table.

"Wasn't she wonderful?" Eve raved. "She stepped in just like an old pro. I'm so proud."

"Oh, so am I," Amy said. "This is our cousin, Robin. Robin, this is Eve Sendry. You might remember her as Kitty McAllen from school."

"Yes, I do remember," Robin said, shaking the hand Eve offered. "I saw some of the plays you and Tracy were in. But where is she?"

Eve frowned. "She wasn't with us in the curtain call? I didn't even notice. She must be backstage." She smiled. "I'm going to scold her for that. She definitely deserved to take a bow, and she shouldn't be shy about it. I'll get someone to go find her, okay? I'm still supposed to be mingling."

"That would be great," Amy said.

"I'll take care of it."

Eve went over to one of the ushers, said something to him, and then went to visit with the people sitting at another table. The room was filled with chatter and laughter. Over the next little while, the audience thinned out, the actors told everyone good night and went to change out of their costumes, and the staff came to clear the tables, but still there was no sign of Tracy.

"We'd better go see what's keeping her," Amy said finally, and she and Robin headed toward the stage.

Before they got very far, Eve rushed up to them.

"The usher I sent to look for Tracy hasn't found her. I've had everybody searching backstage, but she's gone. She's just gone."

Chapter Four

*G*one?" Amy glanced at Robin and then back at Eve. "How can she be gone?"

"I don't know." Eve was in tears. "We've looked everywhere. Her purse and her clothes are still in the dressing room where she changed. Her phone and her keys are still there too."

Robin's face was suddenly pale. "I'll go see if her car is still here."

"Okay." Amy squeezed her hand. "I'll see what I can find out backstage."

She followed Eve to the dressing room. Sure enough, as Eve had said, all of Tracy's belongings were right where she must have left them. A quick check of her purse showed that there was still cash and credit cards in it.

"Where could she have gone? What about the rest of the boat?" Amy was nearly frantic.

Eve wrung her hands. "I don't know. I don't know. Danny's got some of the crew searching the upper level. Devlin, he played Lord Melbry, is checking the cabins. Everybody else is looking wherever they can."

"But didn't anybody see anything?" Amy felt tears burn her eyes. "She wouldn't have just left, and if she had, wouldn't somebody have seen her? Danny's the stage manager. Wouldn't he have been watching everybody's entrances and exits?"

"Most of the time, but Tracy's exit is at the end of the act. He would have been at the other end, making sure the hands were ready to change the set as soon as the curtain went down. And I usually exit through the door in the middle of the stage, not at the side, where Tracy and Calvin were."

Amy drew a sharp breath. "Where's Calvin? I didn't see him at the curtain call either. Have you seen him?"

Eve gaped at her for a moment. "No. I don't suppose I have. I don't usually pay that much attention, but I don't think he was there. You don't think he—" She looked frantically around the dressing room and then hurried out into the corridor. "Has anybody seen Calvin lately? Anybody?"

No one had.

"Did you find her?" Robin asked, rushing into the corridor from the theater. "Her car's still here."

"Nothing," Amy said. "Oh, Robin, she's just gone."

Danny came up behind Robin, his expression taut. "You ladies better come with me."

"What is it?" Amy asked, as she, Robin, and Eve scurried after him. "Did you find her?"

He led them behind the stage and up to a group of deck-hands who were gathered around what looked like a storage closet. Calvin lay on a blanket at their feet as one of them cut away the black electrical tape that bound his wrists and ankles. Another piece of the same tape dangled from the corner of his mouth.

"I'm okay. Really." He pulled the piece of tape away from his face and, with help, sat up. "I don't know what happened. Right before I was supposed to get behind the screen, somebody came up behind me and threw this blanket over my head. There must have been two of them. One of them said he had a gun. They taped me up and blindfolded me, and the next thing I knew, I was in the closet. I thought nobody would ever find me." He pressed his lips into a hard line. "It's not a very good joke, if you ask me. I guess somebody took over my part?"

"What did they say?" Danny asked.

"Almost nothing," Calvin said. "When they first grabbed me, one of them said, 'Don't make a sound. I've got a gun.' You can bet I believed him."

"That was all?"

"That was all. I didn't recognize his voice. Neither of them said anything else."

"What about Tracy?" Amy asked, kneeling beside him.

"Tracy? What do you mean?"

"Tracy is missing," Eve said. "Did you see her when you went to the stage entrance?"

"I didn't make it to the stage entrance," Calvin told her. "I think whoever got me must have been in this closet or behind one of the sets or something. I was headed that way, and then suddenly I was here. I guess everybody else was at the other end of the stage getting ready to change the set for the next act."

"Where could she be?" Robin asked, clutching Amy's hand. "What are we going to do?"

"Call the police," Amy said, feeling her throat tighten. "The sooner they get here, the more likely it is that we'll find some useful evidence. Maybe you ought to call Terry."

"What about Jeff?" Robin asked.

"I don't know how soon we can reach him and Chad where they are. They probably can't get back here right away anyway. Let's get the police out here first."

The responding officer was Sergeant Dale Leewright. He'd been a friend of Amy's since they were in high school and, except for Tracy's husband, there was nobody she would have rather seen. She went to him almost at a run.

"What's going on?" he asked, his eyes full of concern. "Dispatch said there was a probable kidnapping on board."

Amy nodded shakily, and he took her arm.

"Why don't we sit down, and you can fill me in?"

By then everyone was gathered around backstage, talking in low, worried whispers. Between Amy, Robin, and the better part of the play's cast and crew, Dale was inundated with information.

"Okay, hang on, everybody," he said finally. "Danny, you said you're the stage manager here, right?"

Danny stood behind Eve, clutching the back of her chair. "Yeah, that's right."

"I'll need you to make a list of everybody who's on the boat right now along with their phone numbers and who they are—crew, actor, deckhand, whatever."

"Okay, sure."

"And as best as you remember, write down the name of anybody who was here during the play but isn't around right now. I mean people who work here."

"Got it," Danny said.

"The rest of you," Dale said, "unless you have information that applies to Tracy Doyle or what might have happened to her, please go to your cabin or somewhere else on the boat. Make sure Danny has you on his list before you leave. Thanks. Danny, I'll need you back here when you're done."

"Okay." Danny raised his voice. "Over here, everybody who doesn't have something to tell the officer."

He started herding people out, but Dale stopped him.

"One more thing. All of you should be on the lookout for any evidence that might be related to the kidnapping. Anything out of place. Anything damaged or moved that might show signs of a struggle. Anything that would indicate some unauthorized person was in the non-public areas of the boat. If you notice anything, be careful not to disturb the area, and let Danny know. He'll get back to me with it, okay?"

There was a general murmur of agreement, and then Danny started shooing everyone out again. "Get moving now. Let the man do his job. You can all talk somewhere else. Make sure I have your name down before you go."

Finally, only Amy, Robin, Eve, Calvin, and the deckhands who had found him were left to talk to Dale. All of them told him everything they could about the situation, why Tracy was on stage that night, and why no one had missed her or Calvin earlier.

"And nobody outside the family or the company here knew Tracy was going to be in the play tonight?" Dale asked, still taking notes about what they'd said so far.

Amy wiped her hand over her eyes, unable to believe this was really happening. "Her family is out of town for Labor Day. I told my kids and a friend of mine and his kids, but that's all. Oh, and my neighbor who's looking after my kids for me."

"I told my husband and son," Robin said, "but I don't think they would have mentioned it to anyone. I didn't know till yesterday. It all happened so fast." Her voice broke. "We thought it would be something fun for her to tell everybody when they got home."

Amy squeezed Robin's hand, trying hard to keep her emotions under control, sending up a constant prayer that God would show them what to do and protect Tracy wherever she was.

"Tracy still writes for the newspaper, doesn't she?" Dale asked.

Amy nodded.

"Is there a particular story she's working on? Something that might upset anyone?"

"I don't think so. She's doing something on some of the people we went to school with, like Eve here, but it's just a human-interest piece. Nothing that would upset anyone. Mostly about people who went on to do something interesting or be successful in some way after graduation."

"Nothing somebody might want kept quiet?"

"Nothing," Amy said. "She told me there was one guy in our class that got himself in trouble over some kind of stock fraud in New York, but he died in 9/11. I don't think he even has any family or anybody who would care about that being in an article now. It's not like what he did would be news to anyone who wanted to look him up in the past twenty years. And she hasn't even written the article yet. How would anybody know what was going to be in it?"

"Okay. Can either of you think of any reason at all that someone would want to take Tracy? Any threats? Any arguments with anyone in business? A neighbor? Even the slightest little thing?"

Amy and Robin both shook their heads.

"Did anyone in your family recently come into money?" Dale asked.

"No," Amy said. "Not that I heard of anyway, and I think Tracy would have told me if she knew of anything. She and Jeff are comfortable, but it's not like they have enough money to make someone want to hold her for ransom."

"And why would the kidnapper pick her over anyone else?" Robin asked.

"That's what I'm trying to find out," Dale said. "Has Tracy acted strange recently? Upset? Worried?"

"No," Amy said. "She was happy that she would have the house to herself for a couple of days so she could get her article written, but I know she was looking forward to having her family back tomorrow too."

"Where did they all go?" Dale asked.

Amy gave him the details she had, particularly on where Jeff was. "Should we try to reach him and her son? They're due back tomorrow, but I don't know if they even have cell service where they are."

"We can have officers try to find them," Dale said. "It's your call."

"Jeff's going to be so upset," Robin murmured. "And every-body else."

"I'm so sorry," Eve said, rummaging in the pocket of her costume gown and pulling out a tissue. "I feel partly to blame for this. I should never have asked her to fill in. I thought it would be fun for her and for me."

Dale looked her way. "Tell me again how you happened to arrange for her to be in the play."

Eve repeated what she had already said, sometimes stumbling over her words under his inscrutable gaze, but except for adding a few details, not changing anything.

"You knew you were going to be in her newspaper article?" Dale asked.

Eve nodded.

"Did that upset you?"

Eve blinked at him and gave a low, incredulous laugh. "Of course not. We were friends. She interviewed me for her article, and it was going to be very nice, very flattering. Certainly nothing I wouldn't want published. Publicity always helps in our business. What did she tell you, Amy? She didn't have any plans to do something different, did she?"

"Not at all," Amy said. "She was eager to write about your career since you left Canton. It certainly wasn't going to be anything unflattering or critical."

Eve laid a hand on her heart. "I don't know how it could be. To be honest, I haven't exactly had the most illustrious acting career, but there's nothing particularly juicy for anyone to dig up."

"So it was supposed to be a puff piece," Dale said.

"I don't know if I'd call it that exactly," Amy said. "But from what she told me, it was only meant to be something her readers might enjoy, especially Canton's long-time residents. Nothing that would make anybody commit a felony to keep it out of print." She wiped her eyes again and took a deep, steadying breath. "I'm sorry, but I need to call my neighbor and see if my kids can spend the night with her. I should have picked them up by now."

"Sure," Dale said, compassion in his expression. "I'll talk to Calvin for a few minutes. You take your time."

"Want me to come with you?" Robin asked when Amy stood up to move to the other side of the room.

"Yeah, I do. This seems so surreal. I can't believe I have to tell Deb that Tracy's been kidnapped."

Robin bit her lip. "What about the kids? What are you going to tell them?"

Amy squeezed her eyes shut. "I can't deal with that tonight. Actually, I don't think I'm even going to tell Deb what's happened. I'm going to ask her if Matt and Jana can stay the night and tell her I'll explain everything in the morning. The kids are probably already asleep by now anyway, and I don't see any reason to upset them."

"What about Sara and the rest of Tracy's family?"

"I'll call Jeff," Amy said after a moment's consideration. "He can decide who else ought to know tonight. Do you think you ought to call Terry?"

"Yeah. I'd feel better if he was here. Kai's friend invited him and some other guys over for an all-night movie marathon, and I think I'll leave him be. I know he's almost fifteen now, but I can talk to him about this tomorrow. I don't want him coming up here with Terry. It's hard enough to deal with this as an adult."

They each got on their phones. Jeff was evidently somewhere with no reception, so Amy had to leave him a message to call her. Deb said it was no problem for Matt and Jana to stay with her overnight and that she hoped Amy's sudden difficulty would be quickly resolved. Terry told Robin he'd be at the *Lucky Chance* right away. Afterward, Amy and Robin went back to where Dale was still interviewing Calvin and Eve. Evidently nothing they had said to him was proving very helpful at this point.

"It's early yet," Dale told Amy and Robin.

Calvin looked at them apologetically. "I wish I knew something else to tell you. Except for when the guy said he had a gun, I didn't hear anything. They put a blindfold over my eyes, so I never saw anything either." His faint laugh was low and unsteady. "I don't think I've ever been so scared in my life."

Amy wrapped her arms around herself, trying to keep calm. What was Tracy going through right now? Where was she?

"I've got your list," Danny said when he returned a few minutes later. He handed Dale a lined yellow pad with the name, phone number, and job of everyone on the boat written in large, clear capitals.

"Thanks," Dale said, tearing the written-on pages out of the pad. "Now, would you please show me exactly where Tracy was when she was last seen?"

Just as they were going backstage, Terry hurried into the room. "Robin?"

With a soft cry, Robin ran to him and threw herself into his arms, hiding her face against his chest. "This is so awful."

"I know," he murmured. "Are you okay?"

Robin nodded against him.

"Are you okay, Amy?" he asked.

"Not really," Amy admitted, suddenly wishing she had someone she could cling to right now. She was grateful when Terry put his arm around her shoulders.

"Any new developments?" he asked Dale.

"In the play, she was supposed to be abducted from behind a screen," Dale said. "We were just going to go look there. They might have left some evidence behind."

Danny led everyone to the stage and explained how the scene was supposed to work and why no one missed Tracy until after the show was over.

Dale studied the screen and the stage entrance behind it. "I suppose people have been in and out of here since her exit."

"Yes," Eve told him. "Several of us enter and exit through here during Act Three."

"I'm going to have the stage closed off to everyone until I can get a forensic team in here," Dale said.

"Okay," Danny said. "We're dark tomorrow. Nobody needs to be in here anyway."

"Let's do that now. Why don't you show me where you found Calvin."

"Right."

When they reached the storage closet behind the stage, Dale shook his head. "From what you've told me, some of the deckhands found Calvin in here. Is that right?"

"I'm glad they did," Calvin said gravely.

"So they opened the door and pulled you out."

"That's right."

"There might not be much we can get from here either, after all that traffic." Dale turned to Danny once more. "I want this locked up too."

"Yeah, sure." Danny immediately took out a ring of keys, found the right one, and locked the closet door.

"What now?" Amy asked, feeling as if she was going to be sick. "What can we do?"

Dale took her arm and walked with her back to the dressing room, where Tracy's purse and clothes still were. "Is there anything about her things that seems out of place to you? Anything at all?"

Amy shook her head. "Nothing."

"I told everyone not to touch anything," Danny said.

"This is off-limits too," Dale said. "I want everybody out of here and this room secured."

Everybody trooped out to where the audience had been seated for the performance. The room looked grim and stark now that the tables had been stripped and the chairs stacked against the walls. Dale kept walking until everyone was in the lobby and Danny had locked the dining room.

"I want you to go home now, Amy," Dale said. "Try as best as you can to get some sleep. Terry, you take Robin home. I'm going to get a team out here, and we'll find out what happened to Tracy as quickly as possible."

"Yes, you should," Eve said, taking Amy's hand.

Amy shook her head, her breath coming more quickly. "I can't leave. I couldn't possibly sleep. We've got to find her. I don't understand why anybody would want to take her in the first place. She was just—"

"Officer!" One of the deckhands ran up to Dale and grabbed his arm. "There's something you ought to see. We were looking for how the woman might have been taken off the boat, and we found something."

"What?" Amy asked.

"One of the lifeboats is missing. We figure she must have been taken over the side in that."

"Which way?" Dale asked, but before the man could answer, Amy's phone rang.

Amy grabbed it, hoping against hope that it was Tracy, but then she sighed. "Not a number I recognize. Probably spam."

She started to put the phone back into her purse, but Dale stopped her.

"It could be the kidnappers."

Amy caught her breath and then answered. "Hello?"

"Amy? Oh, Amy, thank goodness. It's me."

Chapter Five

racy." Amy felt her knees almost buckle beneath her, and she was glad Dale grabbed her arm to steady her. "Tracy, are you all right? Where are you?"

"I'm not exactly sure where," Tracy said with a shaky laugh that was almost drowned out by loud music and the sounds of talk and laughter. "I'm in some kind of biker bar on the riverfront. Um, a place called—"

Between the pandemonium in the bar and the rapid-fire questions from everyone around her, Amy couldn't hear what Tracy had said.

"Wait a minute, wait a minute," she said, waving one hand to still the people on her end of the line. "I'll put her on speaker." She pressed a button on her phone, and rock music immediately blared from it. "Can you hear me, Tracy?"

"Yes," Tracy said. "Can you come get me?"

"Tracy, where are you?" Robin asked. "What happened?"

"We can come get you," Terry said. "What's the name of the bar?"

"It's called Flotsam and Jetsam," Tracy said, shouting to be heard. "Wait. Their address is on the matchbook."

The bar was on the opposite side of the river, a little way to the south. Dale wrote it down.

"Tracy, what happened?" Eve said. "We've been so worried about you. Poor Calvin was tied up and—"

Dale held up one hand to stop her. "Tracy, this is Dale Leewright. Are you safe where you are?"

There was the sudden crash of what sounded like shattering glass and then raucous laughter from Tracy's end of the line.

"Yes," Tracy said. "I'm all right, but I really want to go home."

"Okay, stay put. I'm heading your way."

"*We're* heading your way," Amy said as two police officers rushed into the lobby.

"I'll be waiting for you," Tracy said. "Hurry."

"We're coming now," Amy assured her.

Dale beckoned to the officers. "You see to things here," he said to them. "Find out from the deckhands where the missing lifeboat was stored and keep everybody away from the area. You can send everyone home for the night, but let them know not to leave town."

"Let me get my purse," Eve said. "I'm coming with you."

"You stay here," Dale told her. "Right now, we're having family only."

Eve responded with a disappointed huff as Amy, Terry, and Robin followed Dale out to the parking lot. Dale used his radio to call his dispatcher to arrange for a forensics team, and then he drove them out to the bar where Tracy waited.

Flotsam and Jetsam was pretty much what Amy expected—a low, tin-roofed building with a gravel parking lot and rows of motorcycles outside. The name of the place flashed in hot-pink neon above a wide wraparound porch that was packed with boisterous patrons.

"I'll go get her," Dale said when he pulled his patrol car up to the front door. "All of you stay put."

It was a rough-looking crowd, but apart from a few wary glances from a couple of men, Dale's presence went unnoticed. He came out a moment later with Tracy beside him, a little unsteady, her costume from the play rumpled and her makeup smeared. A pair of burly, tattooed men made way for her through the crowd.

Tracy stopped to say something to them before she and Dale continued to the car.

"Tracy!" Amy threw open the door and rushed to hug her sister. "Oh, thank goodness."

Terry got out of the back seat. "You three girls sit together. I'll sit up front."

"Thanks," Tracy said. She returned his hug and then got in the car.

Amy got in beside her. "Are you sure you're all right?"

"We were so worried about you," Robin said, taking Tracy's hand. "You're not hurt, are you?"

"No," Tracy assured them. "A little bruised, maybe, but that's mostly from trying to work myself loose. I'm just glad it's over and, to be honest, pretty mad that this even happened."

"I would have been terrified," Robin said.

"Oh, believe me, I was," Tracy said. "But then I realized I'd been dumped."

"What do you mean you were dumped?" Dale asked. "How did you get away?"

"As far as I can tell, they let me go."

"Who let you go?" Amy asked. "What did they say?"

"And by they," Dale added, "do you mean there was more than one person?"

"There were at least two," Tracy said. "And they didn't say anything. I mean, except for when they first took me. I stepped behind the screen and screamed, thinking that was Calvin standing there with his back to me, but then I realized that whoever was there wasn't Calvin. He threw a blanket over my head and told me to keep quiet or he'd shoot me."

"Were those his exact words?" Dale asked.

"Let me think," Tracy said. "As best I can remember, he said, 'Keep quiet. I have a gun.' Then they put a blindfold over my eyes and taped my mouth and my wrists and ankles and carried me outside."

"Did you recognize the man's voice?" Amy asked.

"I didn't," Tracy said. "But he could have disguised it."

"What happened after they carried you outside?" Dale asked.

"They put me in a small boat. I never heard a motor, so I guess they rowed it. It wasn't very long before we docked somewhere and they lifted me out and took me inside someplace with a door and put me down on the floor—I found out later it was a boathouse."

"And then?"

"Then nothing. We just waited. It's hard for me to say how long it was. Finally, I heard a car outside. The door opened, and somebody came in. I heard whoever it was come close to me, and I was sure something awful was going to happen, but after a few seconds, that person and the two men who had taken me walked away."

"They left?" Amy asked.

Tracy shook her head. "I could hear them talking, but I couldn't tell what they said. They sounded like they were about ten feet away.

One of them sounded pretty angry. After a minute or two, one of them walked off, and I heard the door open and slam shut and then a car drive away. Then the other two, I think it was the two who took me in the first place, came back to where I was. My wrists were taped together behind my back, and one of them put something in my hand. Then he and the other guy walked away."

Dale glanced at her in the rearview mirror. "What did they say?"

"Nothing," Tracy said. "I heard the water, like they were getting in the boat again, and then everything was quiet."

"What did they give you?" Amy asked, unnerved by the whole thing.

"I wasn't sure at first, but then I realized it was a pocketknife. It was open, and I was afraid I would cut myself, but I finally got through enough of the tape so I could get my wrists free. I pulled off my blindfold and the tape over my mouth and then cut the tape on my ankles. The only light came from the moonlight coming from the open door. I had heard the sounds of water, but I wasn't sure before whether it was a boathouse or maybe an actual house with a dock. I was afraid one of the kidnappers might still be around, but nobody was nearby. I started walking down the road and finally saw lights and heard music. That was the bar I called you from."

Dale looked into the rearview mirror again. "How far do you think you walked?"

"I'm not sure. I don't think it could have been more than a mile or so. The bar was on my right when I came to it. I'm not sure what direction I was going."

"You would have come from the north then," Dale said. "I'm sure we can find that boathouse pretty easily. Once you've had a chance to get cleaned up and get some sleep, we're going to have to have you come identify it for us."

"Sure," Tracy said. "I can lead you right to it. The walk from there was something I'll never forget."

"I'm glad that bar wasn't too far away," Terry said.

"Me too. And they were really nice. I must have looked strange walking up there dressed like Miss Marple, but those two men who walked out with me, Dave and Benny, helped me inside and got me a glass of water to drink and then let me borrow a phone to call you." Tracy smiled a little. "Benny wanted to get a bunch of his friends to take their bikes up the road to see if they could find the men who kidnapped me. I told him the police would handle it."

"Good," Dale said half under his breath.

"It must have been scary walking down that dark road in the middle of the night," Robin said.

Amy felt Tracy shiver.

"At least there was enough of a moon for me to see the way," Tracy said with a faint laugh. Then she rubbed her eyes and drew a shaky breath. "I don't know when I've been more afraid."

"Oh." Amy put her arms around her sister. "I'm so sorry. We're just glad to have you back."

Tracy sniffled. "Jeff isn't going to want me to leave the house alone ever again. He must be worried sick."

"We haven't told him anything yet," Amy said. "I left a message for him to call me, but he must be out of range somewhere."

"Oh, good," Tracy said. "Since this turned out to be nothing, I wouldn't want to spoil everybody's trips. I'll call him and tell him not to worry, and then I'll catch him up when he gets home."

"I wouldn't say it was nothing," Dale said. "We still don't know who's behind it or what the motive might be."

"Have you thought about who might want to kidnap you?" Amy asked Tracy.

Tracy exhaled. "I've been asking myself that the whole time. I can't think of any reason someone would want to. It's really strange. And it's even stranger for them to suddenly let me go. They didn't hurt me. They didn't threaten me. They didn't ask for anything. It doesn't make sense."

"We'll figure it out," Amy soothed.

"You let the department handle it," Dale said. "I don't want anybody getting into trouble over this. We don't know enough yet. Tracy could still be in danger."

"I'll be extra careful," Tracy told him. "Though I don't know what more I could have done to be safer than being in a whole theater full of people."

"Somebody had to have known exactly where Tracy was going to be," Amy said, "and the exact moment she and Calvin would each have been alone."

"Oh, what about Calvin?" Tracy asked. "Why wasn't he where he was supposed to be? Is he all right?"

"He had a similar experience," Dale said. "Ended up in a storage closet backstage. He's all right."

"I'm glad he's okay," Tracy said. "He seems like a good guy."

"Why don't you come stay with me tonight," Amy suggested. "Or let me stay with you. I want to make sure you're still around when Jeff and Chad get home tomorrow."

"Why don't you both come stay with me and Robin," Terry said, looking back over the front seat to see Robin's reaction. "What do you think, honey?"

"That's a great idea," Robin said. "I'd feel a lot better if you would."

"But what about Matt and Jana?" Tracy asked.

"They're at Deb's for the night," Amy told her. "I've already arranged that."

"But my purse and my clothes are still at the theater," Tracy protested.

"And your car," Amy said. "And mine."

"I'm taking you all back there," Dale said, "but you need to come into the station as soon as you're able and give us official statements. I've got enough to work with for tonight."

"Look," Amy said, "why don't Robin and Tracy come to my house? I have plenty of room."

"I think I'd like that best," Tracy said. "We'll be fine there, Terry. I promise."

"If you say so," Terry said. "But if you feel uncomfortable by yourselves, give me a call. I can be right over."

Tracy squeezed his arm. "We'll be all right."

Once Dale had retrieved Tracy's belongings and assured them that the department would do everything possible to find out what had happened and why, Robin, Tracy, and Amy got into their cars and headed to Amy's house.

Once there, Robin ran a bath for Tracy and Amy put them all at ease by going around and making sure all the doors and windows were secure.

"If they're still searching for Tracy at this point," she said, "they probably won't look here. But everything's shut up tight, just in case."

"Thanks," Tracy said, and then she yawned. "Oh, sorry. That one kind of snuck up on me."

"You need to get some sleep if you can," Robin said. "Come take your bath."

"You can borrow something of mine to sleep in," Amy added. "We'll swing by your house in the morning for some fresh clothes before we go to the police station."

Tracy nodded and yawned again.

Amy took her arm. "Come on, before you fall down."

Soon Tracy was fast asleep in the guest room and Robin and Amy were at the table in the kitchen, drinking herbal tea.

"I don't know if I'll be able to get to sleep tonight," Robin said.

"Me neither," Amy agreed.

"Thanks for letting us stay. I would have worried about both of you if you were alone. I wish I could figure out who would want to kidnap Tracy. It doesn't make sense."

"Maybe they didn't mean to get Tracy in the first place," Amy said. "Otherwise, why would they just let her go without making any demands or harming her in any way?"

"Whoever did it had to have known about her role in the play," Robin said, clasping her mug in both hands. "That would make you think someone in the play was behind it."

Amy nodded. "She went through her lines and blocking yesterday and had a dress rehearsal right before the audience arrived. Everybody involved in the show saw her. They knew she wasn't someone else." She took a sip of tea, letting the warmth soak into her body and soothe her jangled nerves. "You don't suppose somebody thought she was the girl who went to be a bridesmaid, do you?"

"It's possible," Robin said. "But, again, it seems to me that anybody in the cast or on the stage crew would have known she left and that Tracy took her place."

Amy sighed. "True."

"What about the deckhands and the food service workers?" Robin asked. "Could it be one of them?"

"They wouldn't know that much about how the play works, exactly where Tracy would have been and when," objected Amy. "The same with Calvin. I think we can rule them out."

"I guess you're right," Robin said. "That doesn't leave many people who could have been involved."

Amy frowned. "The only reason I can think of for anyone to actually want to kidnap Tracy is that article she's working on, and Eve is the only one in the play who's going to be in that."

"She could have hired somebody to do it," Robin said.

"But she has no reason to do that. Tracy already told her what the article was going to be like. Very flattering to her and good promotion for the play and the showboat in general."

"Is Tracy working on another article? Something a little more hard-hitting? Something someone wouldn't want coming out?"

Amy shook her head. "Nothing that involves anyone connected with the show. Not that she's told me about anyway."

"Why don't we get some sleep and talk about this again in the morning," Robin suggested. She pushed her chair back and stood. "Maybe Tracy can give us a little more information once she's rested, and we'll all be thinking more clearly."

Amy stood too. "That's a good idea. I feel like I could get some sleep now."

She gathered their cups and put them in the dishwasher. Then she walked with Robin to Jana's room.

"Make yourself comfortable," Amy said. "I'm sure Jana won't mind if you snuggle up with her dolls. I've brought you a pair of my comfy pants and a T-shirt too."

"Thanks," Robin said. "See you in the morning."

Amy went up to her own room and changed into a comfortable sleep shirt. She lay down, listening to the quiet night sounds, the singing of a few late crickets, and the sigh of the wind in the trees. For several minutes, every sound, no matter how slight, made her tense up and wonder if someone was outside looking for a way to get in.

She had only one low light burning beside her bed, and she didn't want to turn it off. She knew it was silly, but she couldn't quite make herself do it. She couldn't dismiss the thought that something truly terrible could have happened to Tracy.

No, that wasn't the right way to think. Instead of imagining the worst, she should be thanking God that Tracy was home and unharmed and that she had been gone only a short time, no matter how frightening that time had been for her and everyone else.

"Thank You, God, for bringing her home safe," she whispered, suddenly feeling drowsy. "Help us find whoever is responsible so nobody else will be hurt."

Her eyelids started to close, but before they shut all the way, she reached over and turned out the light, smiling to remember that God watched over her and over them all. Tomorrow would be soon enough to start investigating what had happened on the *Lucky Chance.*

✦ *Chapter Six* ✦

*A*my woke the next morning to the smell of pancakes, sausage, and fresh coffee. Who was the cook? Robin or Tracy? Not that it mattered. The only thing better than a homestyle breakfast was a homestyle breakfast she didn't have to cook herself.

Amy took a quick shower and got dressed, knowing they'd all have to head to the police station before long. Before she joined the others in the kitchen, she called Deb to explain what was going on.

"I'd rather you not tell Matt and Jana anything about this," she said to Deb once she had described the events of the night before. "I'll talk to them about it when we get home. Just tell them everything is fine, but there's something Aunt Tracy and I have to take care of before I can come get them."

"I'll do that," Deb said. "And I'm happy to keep them as long as you need me to. I'm really glad that Tracy is okay. That had to be scary."

"It definitely was, but everything is okay now, and the police are investigating. Thanks for being so great about taking care of the kids for me. It's certainly not what I expected to happen when I left them with you."

"Really, it's not a problem. I was hoping they'd spend the night in the first place. Gabe is in there letting them help him make what he calls his world-famous breakfast casserole, and they're having a blast. I'll tell them you called and that you'll pick them up in a little while."

"Thanks, Deb, and bless you!"

"Anytime, honey."

After breakfast, Terry picked up Amy, Robin, and Tracy and drove them to the police station. Amy had let Dale know they were on their way, and he was there to meet them, ready for Tracy to show him the boathouse where she had been taken and abandoned the night before.

Soon they passed Flotsam and Jetsam. The bar looked like a ghost of its nighttime self, quiet and lonely, just an empty building with an empty parking lot. Good thing people were there when Tracy needed help.

"I don't think it's much farther up the road," Tracy said once they passed the bar. "It's on the left in some trees."

"I looked at a map of this area earlier," Dale said. "If it's the boathouse I'm thinking of, then I have the owner's name. If it's somebody you know, that might explain everything right off the bat."

Amy glanced at Tracy. Did they know someone who would do such an awful thing? It didn't seem possible. Tracy looked a little unsettled by the idea too.

"There," she said when the road curved to reveal the back of a small boathouse. It was painted a rusty red and had white trim. It looked well cared for.

"You're sure?" Dale asked her.

"Yes. Very sure."

"Good. This is the place I looked up earlier."

Everyone got out of the squad car and went up to the boathouse.

"I don't see anybody around," Dale said, scanning the area. "No cars."

The door stood partly open. A broken padlock hung from the bolt over the doorknob.

Dale examined it without touching it. "This looks like a fairly new lock. Was it this way last night?"

"I don't know," Tracy said. "The door wasn't locked when I tried it. All I did was push it open and get out as quick as I could. I didn't look back."

"I don't want anybody to touch anything, all right?" Dale said, pushing the door open with the toe of his boot.

It was dim inside, and Dale turned on his flashlight and shone it around. There was no boat, but there was a place for one. There were some lockers along one wall and some fishing gear, but not much more than that.

"Was there a boat here last night?" he asked Tracy.

"It was hard to see, it was so dark, but I don't think so. At least not when I left."

"Could you tell if the boat you were in came in here? Or did they tie it up outside?"

"They tied up somewhere and then carried me a ways to where they put me down, so I doubt the boat was in here."

The flashlight caught something shiny, and Dale walked over to it. Then he turned to Tracy. "Come over here a minute. Everybody else, stay where you are."

Tracy went over, looked at what was in the circle of light, and then nodded. "I'm sure that's it."

"Okay, let's get going."

The two of them came back to the door where everyone else waited.

"What is it?" Amy asked.

"The pocketknife they gave me," Tracy said. "And the electrical tape I cut off."

They all went back outside and waited while Dale called for someone to come document everything at the scene.

"We'll have to wait till the officer gets out here and takes charge of the scene before we can leave," he said. "We don't want anybody coming up here and removing any evidence. Shouldn't take long."

"Not a problem," Tracy said. "I definitely don't want anything to be tampered with here."

Amy studied the boathouse for a moment. "Now that we know this is the place, I'm curious who owns it."

Dale took a notebook out of his pocket and opened it. "Belongs to a guy named Robert West."

Chapter Seven

*A*my gasped. "Robert West?"

She scanned the area, wondering if Dale had made a mistake and Robert's place was somewhere nearby.

"Are you sure?" Tracy asked. "This is Robert West's boathouse?"

"According to the tax records," Dale said with another glance at his notes. "You know him, don't you?"

"Yes," Amy said. "We've known him for a long time. I can't believe he would do something like this. I can't believe he'd commit any kind of crime at all. He must be about eighty years old."

Dale snorted. "Eighty-year-olds commit crimes too, you know."

Amy bit her lip, remembering when she had last seen Robert. He'd been leaving the *Lucky Chance*, his face flushed with anger, hot words on his lips. *"I'll prove it!"* What was he going to prove? And could that possibly be connected to Tracy's kidnapping?

"I had forgotten about this with everything that's happened since last night," she said, "but Tracy and I saw Robert leaving the *Lucky Chance* on Friday. He'd been talking to somebody in the owner's office. We didn't hear what they were arguing about, but Robert said he was going to prove something. Then he left."

"You both heard him?" Dale asked, his eyes on Tracy.

"We did," Tracy said. "He didn't see us."

"Do you know who he was talking to?" Dale asked.

"We didn't see the person in the office," Amy said. "I just assumed it was Lyle Pinson, the owner, since it was his office."

"But we don't have any proof of that," Tracy was quick to add. "And even if we'd seen the guy, we wouldn't know if it was Lyle Pinson. We've never met him."

"According to the stage manager, Pinson has been out of town since Saturday morning, but he's due back tonight." Dale added something to his notes. "I'll make sure and have a talk with him about this. It's hard to believe there's no connection here."

That was true enough, but Amy still couldn't imagine Robert being part of something like this. Then again, how well did she know him? He was fun to chat with and had always seemed kind and friendly, but her knowledge of him ended there. It wasn't much to testify to in court.

Just then, another officer pulled up to the boathouse. Dale briefly explained the situation to him and then got everyone into his squad car and drove them to the police station. Once there, Amy and Tracy gave statements about everything that had happened the night before, adding, at Dale's request, a description of what they had seen and heard on Friday when Robert West was on the riverboat. After that Terry drove them back to Amy's house.

"You're both welcome to come hang out with us," Robin said.

"I've got to pick up Matt and Jana," Amy told her as she got out of the car. She already had her phone out of her purse. "They're going to wonder where I've been."

Tracy got out too and glanced at her watch. "I ought to try to call Jeff. He and Chad should be heading back by now, and I'm sure they'll have phone service at this point."

"What are you going to tell him?" Amy asked.

"Nothing yet," Tracy said. "Only that I'm eager to have them come home. Anna and the kids should return today too, so I don't think Chad will be at our house much longer than to pick up his car and take off. I want to talk to Jeff about all this before we get the whole family upset."

"Okay." Robin reached out of her car window and squeezed Tracy's hand. "Feel free to come over if you want to while you're waiting for him to get home."

"Thanks for staying with us last night." Tracy leaned in and hugged her. "Thanks for everything, Terry."

"I'm glad to help anytime," he said. "Be safe."

"We will," Amy said.

Terry waited until Tracy got into her car and started it, and then he waved and drove off.

Amy started to call Deb and tell her she was on her way, but instead she walked over to where Tracy was parked and motioned for her to roll down her window.

"Everything okay? I was about to call Jeff."

"I was hoping you would stay at my house until he gets home," Amy said. "Call me silly if you want to, but I'd feel better if you weren't home alone right now."

Tracy chuckled. "To be honest, so would I. You don't mind?"

"Of course not. I'm going to call Deb and then pick up the kids. I'll hurry."

"Okay. I'll call Jeff and see when he expects to be back and ask him to call me when he's almost home."

"Perfect," Amy said. "See you in a few minutes."

They both made their phone calls, and Amy walked the short distance to the Patterson home.

"Mom!" Jana shrieked when Amy came to the door.

She flung herself into Amy's arms and told her all about making breakfast with Mr. Patterson and the boys. Matt and Russ came in from the backyard a moment later, and Matt gave Amy a hug.

"I wondered where you were," he said, a touch of anxiety in his eyes.

"I'm sorry, bud." Amy stroked his hair. "We had some things happen that we weren't expecting. Mrs. Patterson told you that, right?"

Matt nodded solemnly. "I was still wondering."

"Well, we'll talk it all over when we get home. Aunt Tracy's there too, until Uncle Jeff gets home later."

"Oh, good," Jana said, her eyes bright. "We can tell Aunt Tracy about our breakfast casserole."

"Everything all right?" Deb asked Amy quietly.

"Yes," Amy said. "I'll give you a call when I can. For now, I can't tell you how much I appreciate this. Anytime you're in a bind, feel free to call me. I'll be happy to do whatever I can."

Deb gave her a quick hug. "I know it's hard when you're a single mom. You don't have backup sometimes."

"Usually I do, but this time my usual backups weren't available."

Deb smiled. "Call me when you can."

"I will," Amy said. "Come on, kids. Say goodbye to Russ and thank Mrs. Patterson."

"Thank you," Matt said. "See you, Russ."

Russ gave him a playful punch on the shoulder.

"We had a nice time," Jana said to Deb. "And tell Mr. Patterson he's nice."

"I will, sweetie." Deb hugged her. "He'll be glad you think that."

Amy got everyone out the door, and soon they were home. Tracy opened the front door to greet them.

"Hey," she said as the kids ran to her. "How are you two?"

She hugged them, and both kids eagerly told her about their time at the Pattersons' house.

"Go upstairs and get cleaned up and change your clothes," Amy ordered when they were all inside. "Hurry up, and we'll figure out what to have for lunch."

"What are you going to tell them?" Tracy asked when they were out of sight.

"The truth," Amy said. "As gently as possible."

"I suppose they need to hear about it from you instead of from someone else."

"They'll be able to see that you're here and you're all right. That should make it not too frightening for them, I hope."

"It happened," Tracy said. "Even without details, that's frightening enough. For everybody."

They went to the Purple Cow for a late lunch, which delighted the kids and gave Amy a break from having to even think about fixing something. Then, once they were home again, Amy sat Matt and Jana down on the couch on either side of her. Tracy sat in a chair nearby.

"I know you've both been wondering why I didn't pick you up at Russ's last night," Amy said.

Jana nodded. "I started to get a little scared when I woke up and it was morning and you didn't come get us yet."

"Mrs. Patterson told you I called, didn't she?"

She nodded again. "But I was still worried."

Amy knew that both children had lived with uncertainty their whole lives.

"I'm so sorry," she said. "I want you both to know that I'll never, ever leave you unless there's an emergency. And, if there is, I'll make sure you know I'll be with you the very minute I can."

"Was there an emergency last night?" Jana asked, her eyes round.

"I'm afraid so," Amy said. "That's what I want to tell you about. But first I want you to know that it's all taken care of, and everybody is fine. Okay?"

"But what happened?" Matt asked.

"Well, you know Aunt Tracy acted in a play last night," Amy said.

"I wish we went," Jana said. "Was it good?"

"It was very good," Amy said. "She did a great job, and everybody clapped for her a lot. But then there was a problem. At the end of the play, when it was time for all the actors and actresses to take a bow, Aunt Tracy wasn't there."

Matt frowned. "Why not?"

"Well, in the play, Aunt Tracy was supposed to be taken away by one of the bad guys, and when that happened, we thought it was all pretend. But it turned out to be real."

Matt's frown deepened. "Nuh-uh."

"It really did," Tracy said. "I was scared, but the people didn't hurt me, and after a little while they let me go, and Robin and I came here and spent the night with your mom."

"But who took you, Aunt Tracy?" Jana asked. "How come?"

Amy glanced at her sister, afraid it might be difficult for her to go over all this again, but Tracy seemed calm. Maybe it was good for her to talk about it.

"We don't know yet," Tracy said. "But we told the police all about it, and they're investigating."

Jana hugged her. "I'm glad you're all right. Uncle Jeff would be mad if he got home and somebody had you."

Tracy laughed. "I guess he would."

Matt didn't smile. "Do you think somebody will try to get you again?"

"I don't think so, Matt. From what I can tell, it had something to do with me being in that play. Maybe whoever it was meant to take somebody else, and that's why they let me go so quickly. Whatever it was, I don't know of any reason somebody would want to kidnap me."

"Okay," Matt said. "But you need to be careful from now on."

"I certainly will," Tracy assured him. "And I'm sure Uncle Jeff will tell me the same thing."

Matt finally cracked a smile. "Okay."

"Now," Tracy said, "what's this I hear about you and Miles's kids learning to make Grandma Pearl's meat loaf?"

"It's Grandma Pearl's recipe?" Jana asked.

"It had better be," Tracy said. "That's the only kind I allow at my house."

"It's the only kind I make too," Amy said.

"Hey," Tracy said. "What if I come over and help you learn to make meat loaf and all the other stuff too?"

"Can she, Mom?" Jana asked.

"We'll have a lot to do," Matt added. "So we'll probably need help and stuff."

"Okay," Amy said. "I guess. Are you sure you want to be in the middle of a huge mess, Tracy?"

"I can help keep things tidied up while you and the kids are cooking," Tracy suggested. "How would that be?"

"Actually, that would be a huge help. We're planning it for Saturday afternoon. That'll give us plenty of time to make everything and be able to have it cooked by dinnertime." Amy groaned suddenly. "Oh, man."

"What?" Tracy asked.

"I never did check with Miles to find out if his kids would be able to come that day. They may already have plans."

"No, they don't," Jana said.

"How do you know that?" Amy asked her.

"I already told Natalie about it, and she said they could come."

Amy looked at her dubiously. "Did she ask Dr. Miles if it was okay?"

Jana shrugged. "I guess so."

Amy shook her head. "I'd better call Miles and find out right away."

"You'd better," Tracy said. "Come on, kids. I'll beat you at any card game you pick."

Amy smiled as she watched the three of them hurry upstairs to get the cards. Then she got her phone, a surprising touch of excitement fluttering through her. She had wanted someone's arms around her last night when Tracy was still missing. Deep in her heart, she had known whose arms she'd wanted. *But no*, she reminded herself, *we're just friends*. She'd blown the chance she'd had to have something deeper and more permanent. Was it too late?

"This is about the kids right now," she muttered under her breath. "Just call him and tell him about Saturday. It's not a proposal of marriage." She pressed the call button.

"Amy. Hi. How are you?"

Her mouth went suddenly dry at the sound of his voice. "Doing all right," she said, glad the words were steadier than she felt. "How about you?"

"Just fine. Actually, I was about to give you a call."

"Really?"

"Natalie tells me she and Colton are supposed to come over on Saturday and learn how to cook. I assume you know about that."

Amy chuckled. "I do. But I intended to ask you about it before Jana mentioned it to your kids."

"Yeah, well, it seems Natalie forgot to ask me about it until a few minutes ago. And, yes, that's fine. I'll be happy to bring them over. What time?"

They settled the details.

"Thanks for including them," Miles said. "I haven't had much time to teach them to cook, but I think it's an important skill for everybody to have."

"Well, if I'm going to have my kitchen destroyed by my kids, what's two more?"

"True enough," he said with a laugh. "Next time we'll do something over here, okay?"

"I'm sure Matt and Jana would love that." She wasn't quite ready to end the conversation, though there wasn't much more to be said about Saturday. "Uh, how was your family dinner last night?"

"It was good. My great-aunt just turned ninety, and we had a nice celebration for her. She has three great-grandsons around Colton and Natalie's ages, so they had fun playing. What about you? How was the play?"

"Oh, Miles."

"What? What happened?"

She sank into a chair and, even though she hadn't planned to tell him during this particular phone call, she told him all about what had happened the night before.

"It was terrifying," she said at last.

"But Tracy's all right," he said.

"Yes. She's fine. It's really a mystery why they took her in the first place, but it's more of a mystery why they let her go."

"Man," he said, his voice low and taut. "I would have been out of my mind if it was somebody I—I mean, somebody in my family or something. What did Jeff say?"

"He doesn't know about it yet. He and Chad are on a camping trip. Well, they're on their way home from one. They're due back any time now. Tracy hasn't said anything to them yet."

"He's going to be mad about that, I promise you."

"I hope not. She was gone for such a short time, and he was out where he didn't have cell service."

Miles exhaled. "I guess you're right, but he's not going to like it."

"I know. But at least he and Chad don't have to worry about Tracy on the drive home."

After a moment, he said, "Are you okay?"

"Yeah. I don't know when I've been so scared. I'm just so glad it all turned out okay."

"Thank God," he said softly.

"Yes, exactly."

They were both silent.

"Anyway," she said at last, "I'm glad Natalie and Colton will be able to come over on Saturday."

"So am I," he said, his tone lighter now. "Once they learn to cook, I can let them take over kitchen duties once in a while. With supervision, of course."

"We'll keep it simple for now," Amy said, "but I do want to show them how to read a recipe and how to measure ingredients."

"You're the teacher."

"Yes," she said, smiling even though he couldn't see her. "Yes, I am."

"We'll see you on Saturday then." He hesitated for a moment. "And maybe sometime next week I can take everybody out for burgers or something. What do you think?"

"That sounds wonderful. By the time I get to the middle of a school week, I'm usually really ready to *not* cook."

"Okay, well, we'll make definite plans for that soon. Don't get too booked up."

"I won't."

"Good. And, uh, I'm glad you're okay. I mean you and Tracy."

"Thanks," she said. "We are too."

She ended the call, feeling better somehow now that she'd told him what happened to Tracy, now that she'd admitted to being afraid, knowing he understood.

Before Tracy and the kids finished their second game of Kings in the Corners, Jeff called Tracy, eager to get home, eager to tell her all about the fish he and Chad had caught and how a bear had stolen half the food they'd brought along. Tracy urged him to save all the stories for when they were both home and promised to meet him there.

"Now I get to tell him about last night," Tracy said after she ended the call.

Amy hugged her. "He's going to be very happy that you're all right. And I'm sure he'll be upset that he wasn't here with you when it happened."

"Oh, that would have been worse. He couldn't have stopped it any more than I could, and I don't see any reason why we both should have spent the night being terrified."

"True," Amy said. "You know, we haven't had much time to talk about it between ourselves either. I think we ought to talk to Robert West when we have a chance."

"I have a hard time thinking he was behind this."

"Me too, but it was his boathouse. If somebody is using it without his knowledge, he ought to know."

"I imagine he does know about it by now," Tracy said. "Surely the police will want to talk to him, if they haven't already."

"I'm sure." Amy sighed. "Tomorrow's a school day, but what about tomorrow afternoon?"

"What about the kids?"

"I was thinking maybe Robin would let them play at the store for an hour or so. She usually doesn't mind."

"Good. How about four o'clock then?" Tracy asked. "We could meet at the River Queen. He seems to be there a lot."

"It's a good place to start. And that'll give us time to have some coffee and for you to tell me what Jeff says about last night."

"He's not going to want me to leave the house without an armed guard," Tracy said with a chuckle. "But I'm glad somebody cares enough about me to think that." She dug in her purse and got her car keys. "I'll call you tomorrow, and for sure I'll see you at four."

With a little wave, she hurried out to her car and drove away.

Amy was glad Tracy wasn't going home to an empty house, and she was glad they were going to talk to Robert. There was definitely something going on with him and Lyle Pinson, but what could it have to do with Tracy?

Chapter Eight

After school the next day, Amy dropped Matt and Jana off at Robin's antique shop and then drove to the River Queen Café, where Tracy was waiting for her.

"I saw Robert coming out about five minutes ago," she said. "I was afraid we weren't going to get a chance to talk to him, but then a couple of men stopped him, and they all went back inside."

"So he's still here." Amy took a deep breath. "Let's go."

The café was bustling as usual, and for a moment Amy was worried they might not find a spot to sit where they could have a quiet talk with Robert. But then a family at a corner table got up, and the waitress quickly cleared away the dirty dishes.

"Is it all right if we sit here?" Amy asked her.

"Sure," she said. "Let me get a clean cloth to wipe the table."

While they waited, Tracy nodded discreetly toward the opposite side of the room. "He's talking to those two men over there."

"I see him. As soon as the table is ready, you sit down and I'll go see if he'll talk to us."

Tracy looked a little apprehensive. "Okay."

By then the waitress had returned and was wiping off the table.

Amy moved closer to her sister and lowered her voice. "Are you sure you're all right with this? We can leave it totally to the police if you'd rather."

"No," Tracy said. "I mean, it does feel a little bit creepy to wonder if he could be involved, but I'm not going to spend the rest of my life afraid of everybody. I'm ready to do this."

Amy squeezed her arm. "Good."

"You can sit down now," the waitress said. "May I get you something to drink?"

Tracy sat. "Yes. Would you bring us three cups of coffee, please."

"Right away. Are you expecting someone to join you?"

"We hope so," Tracy said.

"I'll be right back," Amy said. She headed toward Robert West's table.

The three men were talking in low, serious tones, but they broke off when she approached them.

"I hope I'm not interrupting anything important, but I wondered, Robert, if you have a minute to come talk to me and my sister."

He nodded. "Manny, Caleb, I'll talk to you later."

He stood up, put some money on the table, and then walked with Amy to where Tracy sat waiting for them.

"I figured I'd hear from one or the other of you," he said in a quiet, strained voice unlike his usual hearty one.

Amy sat across from Tracy and Robert sat between them, his back to the wall.

"I suppose the police have spoken to you," Amy said to him.

Robert nodded. "Like I said, I've been expecting to hear from you two."

"What did they say to you?" Tracy asked.

"Mostly they asked a lot of questions," Robert said. "How do I know you? How long? Where was I Sunday night? Did I usually let people use my boathouse? That kind of thing."

"They must have been satisfied with your answers," Tracy said.

"For now." Robert took the cup of coffee the waitress brought him and added sugar to it. "I'm a person of interest at this point." He looked at Tracy. "Do you think I was behind having you kidnapped?"

Tracy winced. "I don't think so, but I don't know who else to even consider. Why would you want to?"

"I think that's why I'm not in jail right now," Robert said. "The only motive they can come up with for me to kidnap you is pretty flimsy. But I didn't help my case by being seen on the riverboat Saturday night."

"What were you doing on the boat?" Amy asked.

"Who saw you?" Tracy asked at the same time.

"One of the deckhands saw me and said something to the police about it. I was looking for Lyle Pinson, but I guess he's out of town."

"That's what we were told," Tracy said. "They said he'd be in Vegas until sometime last night."

"Tracy and I saw you on the boat Friday afternoon," Amy said, "when you were arguing with somebody in the office. You seemed pretty upset."

"I was," Robert said. "Still am. But that has nothing to do with anybody being kidnapped." His expression softened. "I'm sorry that happened to you, Tracy. I'd like to find whoever's responsible and make sure he never does anything like that again, but it has nothing to do with my beef with Lyle."

"He was the man you were arguing with in the office?" Amy asked.

"Yes. He and I go way back. He always was a slick-tongued rascal. I met him when we were working on the same ferryboat twenty-five years ago. He's only gotten sneakier and greedier since then."

"What did he do?" Amy asked.

He took a big gulp of coffee and then wiped his mouth on his napkin. "He's a greedy one, like I said. We worked on that ferry about seven years together. The captain was Will Finley, a good man, a good sailor. He'd lost his wife, his kids were grown and gone, and the ferry was his whole life."

"So he was an older man," Tracy said.

"Yes." Robert nodded. "I was in my fifties, and I'd say Captain Finley was about ten years older than me. The owner wanted him to retire. He had a good pension coming, but Cap said he wasn't ready. He wasn't ready to quit the river. I know myself, she's not an easy thing to quit."

Robert's passion for the Mississippi and the sailor's life had never been a secret. Amy had always wondered if he had retired voluntarily or if he'd been required to quit once he reached a certain age. Clearly, he and this Captain Finley had been a lot alike.

"What happened with you and Lyle?" Tracy asked.

Robert's mouth tightened. "There was an audit of the ferry operation. They found out that someone had been embezzling for the past four years. They blamed it on Captain Finley because Pinson told them Cap had some cash squirreled away. It was money he'd been saving his whole life. He'd never been much for trusting banks or investments. He always said you couldn't go wrong with hard cash. I knew he was innocent, but the owner needed a scapegoat to keep his investors happy, and Cap was as good as any."

"And you think Lyle was the one who took the money," Amy said.

"I'm sure of it. Some of the so-called evidence against Captain Finley was planted. They found tickets for some racetrack bets that had gone wrong. Cap never placed a bet in his life. He didn't believe in it, but I know somebody who could never stay away from the horses or the bookies."

"Lyle?" Tracy ventured.

Robert sneered. "He's not in Vegas for the shows."

"Did you tell the police all this at the time?" Amy asked.

"I did, but I didn't have any hard evidence against him. Only what I knew about the man from working with him for seven years. Like I said, the owner wanted a quick settlement of the case, and they badgered Captain Finley into taking a plea deal. They gave him fifteen years. He lived eight of those, and every day of it without the sound of water nearby."

"And you're wanting to clear his name," Tracy said.

"If I can." Robert downed the rest of his coffee and put the cup on the edge of the table for the waitress to refill. "I owe it to the captain."

"What's made you bring this up again after so long?" Amy asked.

"I was out on the dock a few days ago, and I heard Lyle was in Canton with his showboat. A couple of hands talked about him losing a lot of money on a local game, and I didn't want him pulling the same trick on one of his men now to make up the money he was out."

"You know," Tracy said, "after all these years, the statute of limitations has probably run out on what he did to Captain Finley. Even if you prove Lyle planted evidence on him, there's not a lot the police can do at this point."

"True." Robert rubbed his stubbled chin. "But if I can prove what he did then, he's not likely to get away with it again. The word is he's hurting for cash right now. He's got to be desperate enough to get it however he can."

The waitress came by and filled their cups again.

"You said the motive the police have for you is flimsy. What kind of motive are they talking about?" Amy asked once the waitress left.

"It's crazy," Robert said with a humorless laugh. "They say I want to hurt Lyle and thought that a scandal would ruin his business."

"Most shows would be thrilled with the publicity," Tracy said. "Especially a showboat with a play about a murder mystery."

"Is there any actual evidence against you?" Amy asked Robert.

"Nothing that's not circumstantial," he said. "That deckhand must not have seen much the night I was there, or the police might have kept me longer than they did."

"What do you mean?" Tracy asked.

"I went into Pinson's office hoping to find something I could take to the police to prove he's a dirty crook."

Amy lifted one eyebrow. "And?"

"Nothing," Robert said. "The only thing I saw that might indicate he needed money was an unopened letter from Decker and Bradley Marine and Aviation."

"Did you open it?" Tracy asked.

Robert snorted. "What, you think I'm crazy? I wasn't there to break the law. The office was open—I didn't even break in."

Amy frowned. "So what made you think that letter meant he needed money?"

"Decker and Bradley is a boat and plane finance company," Robert said. "I'm thinking Pinson financed the showboat through them. The envelope was stamped 'final notice' in red."

"That means he's past due," Amy said.

"It *could* mean that," Tracy said. "It could be something like a refinancing offer or some kind of insurance too."

Amy sighed. "I guess. Is that something you're familiar with, Robert?"

"Not with that company in particular," Robert said, "but I'm assuming it's a demand for payment. He's smart enough to keep anything incriminating out of his office, I expect. Probably wouldn't have left that lying around if he hadn't been out of town."

"But you didn't open it," Amy said. "Did you touch it?"

Robert shook his head. "I only had a look around before I heard someone out in the hallway and thought I'd better get out. Likely it was the deckhand who saw me before and came to see if I was still around."

Amy shook her head. "If you had been caught in the office, I'm afraid you would have gotten yourself into more trouble than you would have given Lyle."

Robert's expression turned hard. "Captain Finley died in prison because of him, and if I can't do anything else, I'm going to make sure he never does that to anybody else."

"We'll see what we can find out about him," Amy said. "And maybe it'll have something to do with the kidnapping too."

"I don't see how," Robert said. "I just know I had nothing to do with that." His smile was warm and genuine. "Pearl's granddaughters? I couldn't hurt either of you any more than I could hurt my own grandson."

"I didn't know you had a grandson," Tracy said.

"Oh, yes ma'am." Robert pulled his wallet from his back pocket and took out a picture of a boy in his early teens holding up a bowling trophy. "That's not very recent, I'm afraid. He's grown now, visiting me and my wife and some friends here for a couple of weeks until his new job starts in St. Louis."

"I'm glad you get to spend some time with him," Amy said.

Robert put the photo back in his wallet. "I know you girls don't know me that well, but I knew your grandma, and if she were still around, I'm sure she'd vouch for me."

"I'm sure she would," Tracy said, giving his arm a squeeze. "I hope you'll forgive us for questioning you about all this."

"Nothing to forgive. Nothing at all," he said, patting her hand. "From what I can tell, it doesn't make sense that anybody would have wanted to kidnap you. I hope the police find something for you soon. That's a real puzzler."

"It is," Tracy said. "But there has to be some evidence that will help us find out who did it and why. And if we get any information about Lyle, we'll be sure to tell you, okay?"

"That'd be just fine." He glanced at his watch and then stood up. "I've enjoyed talking to you both, but I have to get home. Lynn will be waiting for me."

"Lynn. Is that your wife?" Amy asked.

Robert chuckled. "That's my grandson. A family name, and the boy got stuck with it. It's spelled L-i-n, short for Linton."

"Thanks for talking with us," Tracy said. "We'll get in touch if we have any information to share with you."

"I appreciate it."

He reached into his pocket, but Amy stopped him.

"Our treat."

"Oh no."

"But we invited you," Tracy protested.

"Nope." Robert put enough money on the table to pay for the coffees, including a generous tip. "My mother raised me to be a gentleman."

Amy and Tracy both thanked him and, with a wave, he headed out the front door.

"Such a nice man," Tracy said. "I can't imagine him doing anything criminal."

"So we can rule him out, don't you think?" Amy asked.

Tracy gave a somewhat reluctant nod. "Appearances can be deceiving, and we don't know him all that well, but he was a friend of Grandma Pearl's, and there doesn't seem to be a reason for him to want to kidnap me. I think I'm about ninety percent sure he didn't do it. Maybe ninety-five."

"Okay, but we won't rule him out entirely, just in case we learn something that might implicate him."

"Agreed," Tracy said.

Amy thought for a moment. "I wonder about that finance company Lyle may or may not be in trouble with."

"What was it? Something and Bradley?"

"Docker? Decker? Anyway, whatever it is, I think my neighbor Deb's husband might work for them. It sounds familiar for some reason, and I think that's why. I could ask him what that 'final notice' stamp usually means. If Lyle's behind on his payments, that might be worth looking into."

"But it still has nothing to do with the kidnapping," Tracy said. "At least I don't think it does."

Amy nodded. She hoped Robert was who he seemed to be. She sipped her coffee, still speculating about Lyle's money troubles.

"I wonder what Eve knows about him," she finally said. "They have to be a fairly close-knit group, living on the showboat like that. They might not all be great friends, but they probably have some idea about what each other is up to."

"I think we ought to talk to that bookkeeper who's sick," Tracy said. "She probably knows a lot about everybody."

"She might. And Danny. He seems to run things even more than Lyle. He's got to know something. We need to get back over there and have some conversations. Even somebody like Calvin might know something."

"I agree. We need to see what we can find. I hope the police haven't spooked whoever might know something."

"Or who might be in on the kidnapping," Amy said. "But not right this minute. I promised Robin we wouldn't be very long. She's great with the kids, and I told them to be extra good, but I don't want to impose on her too much."

"She won't mind, I'm sure."

"Still, we'd better go. I've got to get dinner ready and see what homework they have tonight."

"You're right." Tracy sighed and stood up. "I need to get back to work on my article anyway. The paper comes out tomorrow, and I want to add something about what happened to me."

"I'm surprised you haven't heard from some of the bigger papers. Surely a kidnapping doesn't happen every day, even in the city."

"Oh, I got a couple of calls last night. I told them I was okay and that I'd be happy to have them print my story as soon as I write it."

Amy grinned. "You want to write all the juicy details yourself."

"No reason I can't give myself an exclusive, is there? And the big papers can afford to pay for my version."

"I'll be interested to see it. Maybe somebody saw or heard something that they'll tell the police about after they see the article."

"I hope so," Tracy said. "We could use a few leads."

Chapter Nine

When Amy and Tracy got to Pearls of Wisdom, they found Matt and Jana sitting at a children's table from the 1950s, playing checkers.

"Are you two ready to go home?" Amy asked.

"Almost," Matt said. "I almost have all the checkers."

"Not yet," Jana said defiantly, moving her last red checker bravely forward.

"Okay," Amy said. "You can finish up."

Robin was dealing with a customer, so Amy took a look around that corner of the shop. There were vintage toys and books and posters, everything decorated for fall.

"Mom used to have this book," she said, thumbing through a primer depicting the adventures of Dick and Jane and their pets, Tip the dog and Mitten the cat.

Tracy nodded. "I remember. Let's see what else Robin has out."

They wandered over to the front counter with its display case, and then Amy looked up and recognized the elderly woman checking out.

"Carol!"

Carol turned around, startled, and then smiled. "Amy. Tracy. How are you?" She took Tracy's hand in both of hers, concern on her gently lined face. "I heard about what happened Sunday night. I'm so sorry. Are you all right?"

"I'm fine," Tracy assured her. "A little shaken up, but okay."

"Evidently word's gotten around Canton about it," Robin said. "I've had several customers ask about you."

"I wish I'd known you were going to be in the play," Carol said. "I would have loved to have seen you in it. It's a fun production, and they serve a wonderful dinner, don't they?"

"You've seen the play?" Amy asked.

"I was there Friday night." There was a gleam of excitement in Carol's eyes. "Don't tell anybody, but I've invested in it. Well, in a group of showboats eventually, but just the one for now."

Amy blinked at her. "Invested? I didn't know that was something you were interested in."

"I hadn't really expected to," Carol said. "I mean, Everett left me a little nest egg when he passed on." She signed the charge slip Robin gave her. "Enough to last me, I think. But I wanted to do something with it, something so I'd have a little money to leave to the grandchildren."

"How did you find out about the investment opportunity?" Tracy asked. "I didn't know they offered interest in the company to the public."

Carol put a hand on Tracy's arm. "Oh no, it's not public at this point. Mr. Daheim—Rudy, I mean—says that might come later, but he gave me a chance to get in on the ground floor. That's what he calls it, anyway. It's like an answer to a prayer."

Amy and Tracy exchanged uncertain glances.

"I hope you checked it out before investing," Amy said.

"Oh, I have," Carol said. "It's all right. I looked Rudy up on the internet. He knows all about theatrical investments. He's a very smart man."

"We met him the other day," Tracy said. "He does seem to know his business."

"Have you talked to your son about this?" Amy asked.

"I want it to be a surprise. He'd want me to spend all the money on myself, but what do I need? My grandchildren, Brent and Sabrina, will be graduating from college before too much longer, wanting to get married and buy houses, I'm sure. They'll need some money to get started with."

"I'm sure they'll appreciate it," Amy said. "I hope it turns out to be a very profitable investment."

"Rudy can't make any guarantees," Carol said, "but I'm sure it will be. I thought everything was first class, and the audience enjoyed it so much."

Amy couldn't help but agree with her. "How did you meet him?"

"Just by chance last Monday," Carol said. "I was having lunch with one of my friends from church, and he backed into me trying to keep from bumping into the waitress. That sloshed my coffee all over my hamburger. He felt so bad, he insisted on ordering me a new one. Well, he was by himself, and Sheila and I couldn't let him eat alone after that, so he sat down with us. We chatted for a while, and when we found out he was involved with the show, we couldn't help asking him about it."

"Sheila Mankus, right?" Tracy said. "Isn't she a widow too?"

Carol nodded sympathetically. "Julian passed away about the same time as Everett. Poor thing, he didn't leave her much. Enough to get by on, but barely."

"We're done, Mom," Matt said as he and Jana came up to the counter. "I won."

Jana frowned at him.

"Okay," Amy said, "but please don't interrupt when people are talking, and say hello to Mrs. Tomlinson."

"Sorry." Matt gave Carol a sheepish smile. "Hello."

"Hi," Jana added.

Carol leaned down a little, her eyes warm. "Hello. Did you have fun playing?"

Both kids nodded.

"We'd better get going," Amy said. "I'm sure some of us have homework to do."

Matt groaned.

"Not me," Jana said, making a face at her brother.

Amy tapped her on her wrinkled nose. "You can help me with dinner."

"It was good to see you, Carol," Tracy said.

"It was nice to catch up with you both," Carol said. "I'm glad you're all right after what happened Sunday night. Will I see you at church this week?"

"We'll be there," Tracy said.

"Absolutely," Amy added.

Robin handed Carol the floral vase she had bought. "Thanks for coming in, Carol. See you soon."

"I appreciate you helping me out with the kids, Robin," Amy said when Carol was gone.

"Did you learn anything helpful from Robert?" Robin asked.

"Not very much," Tracy said.

"I'm sure you'll work it out." Robin came around the counter and hugged Matt and Jana. "You two come back any time you want, okay?"

They nodded eagerly, and Amy took Jana by the hand. "See you soon, Robin."

"Bye, Robin," Tracy said. "We'll talk."

Robin waved. "Got it. Let me know if there's any news."

"I think we need to do a little research on Rudy Daheim," Tracy said as they went out to the parking lot.

"I think that's a good idea," Amy said. "He seems legit enough, I guess, but we don't know anything about him."

"I'm glad Carol had her deal checked out before she invested. Too many older people get scammed out of their retirement money."

They stopped at Amy's car, and Matt and Jana got in the back seat. "It never hurts to be careful," Amy said. "I'd like to know more about him. At least he's not part of Lyle's group."

"Right," Tracy said. "He's definitely been around theater, but he's not an insider on the *Lucky Chance*." She frowned. "I hope Lyle isn't up to something with him. If Lyle's desperate, like Robert says, he might be willing to take whatever money Rudy has to invest and use it to get himself out of trouble instead of putting it into the show."

"I don't know about that," Amy said. "Rudy seems like he knows what he's doing. I get the impression he's been in this business for some time now. But I guess we should still look him up and see what we can find out about him."

"Mom," Matt whined from inside the car, "it's getting hot in here. Can we go?"

"Okay, okay," Amy said. "I'd better go, Tracy. We'll talk later."

"Bye," Tracy said. She gave Amy a hug and walked to her car.

Amy got in and buckled up. "Okay, you two. What do you want for dinner?"

"Pizza!" they chorused.

Amy laughed, not at all surprised.

After dinner, which turned out to be salad, baked chicken, and scalloped potatoes, Amy sent Matt upstairs to do his homework, got Jana to tidy up the army of dolls in her room, and set herself to the task of finding out what she could about Rudy Daheim.

Fortunately, he had a unique enough name that it was easy to find what she was looking for. Daheim Investments, Ltd., was a small company out of New York City. According to the web page, Rudolph Werner Daheim was born in Fort Wayne, Indiana, in 1958, the only child of a German couple who had come to America in 1947. He'd gotten his degree at a satellite campus of Purdue University in Fort Wayne and, after working in the private sector, eventually started his own company, specializing in theatrical investments.

Daheim Investments caters to individual investors interested in promoting excellence in the dramatic arts and in return on investment, the website said. *Contact us for information about our premier investment opportunities.* This was followed by a telephone number and an address in New York City. Besides a contact form and a statement that no investment guaranteed a positive return, there wasn't much more to the website.

"Who's 'we'?" Amy muttered. "Probably a secretary and an accountant in the office to take care of the records while Rudy goes around finding investors. Nice and uncomplicated."

It looked like a small operation, fairly simple. Rudy connected investors with theatrical productions in need of cash. There was no mention of what his cut would be, but presumably potential investors could contact Rudy to find out.

Amy checked the About page again and studied the photo of Rudy. It was a standard studio portrait, fairly recent, with Rudy in a dark suit and tie. He wasn't smiling, but there was something reassuring in his serene expression. She studied the picture and then looked once more at the brief biography.

"1958?" she grumbled. "Why do men age so much better than women?"

There wasn't much to the website at all, so Amy did another search under Rudy's full name. There were some potential listings under a couple of white pages sites, but she didn't want to pay for the privilege of looking at them. She didn't find anything else of note. He'd told the truth when he said he did his work behind the scenes. It was kind of nice to find a man in show business, at least peripherally, who didn't insist on being in the spotlight all the time.

Suddenly remembering the letter Robert had mentioned seeing in Lyle's office, Amy glanced at her watch. It was still early, so she called Deb.

"Hey, Amy," Deb said when she answered the phone. "How are you?"

"I'm fine," Amy said. "Do you have a minute to talk?"

"Sure. How's Tracy doing today?"

"She's doing all right. We'll all feel better when we get a little more information about what actually happened, but at least she's home and safe."

"The police haven't found anything out yet?"

"Not yet," Amy said. "I'm sure these things take time."

"I suppose, but it's got to be maddening to still not know anything."

"They're working on it, and Tracy and I are trying to find out what happened too. Keep that to yourself for now, okay?"

"Oh, sure. No problem. It's very puzzling though." Deb sighed. "Now I'm going to be up all night trying to figure it out."

"If you do, let me know, okay?"

Deb laughed. "Sure."

"There's another reason I called," Amy said. "What's the name of the company Gabe works for?"

"Decker and Bradley."

"Decker and Bradley Marine and Aviation?"

"Yes," Deb said. "Why?"

"I don't want to get into specifics at this point, but could you ask him something for me? Is he home right now?"

"Sure. He and Russ are playing cards and watching a movie."

"I don't want to interrupt anything," Amy said.

"No, it's fine. It's one of those action-adventure things they've seen a hundred times. What do you want me to ask?"

"I know he can't give out information about any particular customer, but could you ask him what it means when an envelope is stamped 'final notice'?"

"Okay. Hang on."

The sounds of shouting and explosions came from Deb's end of the line. Amy could hear her and Gabe talking briefly, and then the battle sounds faded.

"Ugh," Deb said a few seconds later. "I hope that didn't blast you out. Apparently, it's not a good movie if the volume isn't turned all the way up."

Amy chuckled. "At least they're having fun together."

"I'm always up for that. Anyway, Gabe asked if the stamp was in red."

"Yes. It was."

"Okay, he said if it's red, that means somebody hasn't been paying on a loan and whatever was financed is about to be repossessed."

"Oh, wow," Amy said, half under her breath.

"Is this about the kidnapping?" Deb asked when Amy didn't say anything else.

"I don't know. It's all kind of confusing right now, but thanks for asking for me."

"Not a problem," Deb said, sounding as if she'd like to know more.

"I really appreciate your help. I'm not sure what this means as far as what happened to Tracy, if it's connected at all, but it gives us something to check into. Tell Gabe thanks for me. I owe you both."

"I'll do that."

As soon as Deb hung up, Amy called her sister.

"Wait till you hear what I found out," Amy said before Tracy could say anything.

Tracy chuckled. "Well, hello to you too."

"Are you in the middle of something?"

"No. Jeff and I just finished dinner. He hasn't let me out of his sight since he got home, except when he's teaching."

"Not true!" Jeff protested in the background. "I went out to get the mail!"

Amy laughed. "Sounds like he's not planning to let anything happen to you ever again."

"He's been wonderful," Tracy said. "And I've sure been glad to have him here. I don't think I'm going to feel truly safe again until we find out what happened."

"That's what I called about. I found out a couple of things you ought to know."

"Oh, good. I was going to google Rudy, but I haven't had a chance to yet."

"I did that. How old do you think he is?"

"I don't know. Around our age, maybe?"

"He's sixty-five."

"You're kidding," Tracy said. "Really?"

"Really. I thought he was our age too, maybe two or three years older even, but his website says he was born in '58. Usually, a beard makes a man look older than he is, but definitely not in this case."

"Maybe he had a little work done. It's not unusual, even for men, and he probably has the money for it."

"If he did, I'd like to know who his surgeon is, because you sure can't tell."

"I hear they're getting better all the time," Tracy said. "But what else did you find out about him?"

"Not much. He told us he keeps a low profile, and so far that's been true."

"I don't blame him. I wish I could figure out why he seems familiar. It's bugging me."

"Maybe you met a relative of his. A brother or a son."

"Could be," Tracy said. "I did a story on a Broadway show I went to a few years ago. Maybe he was involved with that somehow. You know things like that bother me until I figure them out."

"It's the reporter in you. Or maybe it's why you ended up being a reporter."

Tracy chuckled.

"Anyway," Amy said, "that's not the important part."

"What is?"

"I think I know what was in that letter Robert saw on Lyle's desk."

"Is Lyle about to lose the showboat?" Tracy asked.

"I'm pretty sure that's it. At least that's what Deb's husband says it usually means when they send out a letter with 'final notice' stamped in red."

"So Robert may be right about Lyle being in financial trouble, but that letter doesn't actually prove it. And it probably doesn't have anything to do with the kidnapping. Whoever took me didn't ask for any money."

"I know," Amy said. "But I can't help wondering if the kidnappers got the wrong person, and that's why they let you go so fast."

"I thought that too, but it doesn't make sense. Whoever took me knew the exact time and place when I would be at one end of the stage and everyone else would be at the other end getting ready for the next act, right?"

"Right," Amy said. "That would mean it had to have been a member of the cast or crew."

"Exactly. That's fact number one. Fact number two is, everyone involved with the play knew I was filling in for the bookkeeper.

They knew the wardrobe girl was going to a wedding and that the bookkeeper was sick. We had a dress rehearsal of my scenes earlier that night, and everyone was there. They all knew I was playing Cousin Muriel. So, taking both facts together, the only logical conclusion is that it's someone from the cast or crew, and I was their target."

Amy sank into the comfy armchair next to the fireplace. "I think we should talk to the bookkeeper," she said. "She would've been there that night too. I mean, if she lives on the boat like everybody else, wouldn't she have been there even if she was sick that night?"

"That's true," Tracy said. "And that's another fact that supports my theory that whoever the culprit was, they really did mean to kidnap me. If they'd wanted the bookkeeper, they would have gone to her cabin to get her."

"I think we should go talk to her tomorrow. Are you game?"

"That's a good idea. And Lyle will be back aboard the *Lucky Chance* again too. I'd like to talk to both of them."

"Do you want to meet after school tomorrow and go over there?" Amy asked. "I'm sure Miles would be willing to look after the kids again for a little while."

"Okay, sure. I need to do some work on my 'where are they now' article, but I'll have most of the day for that. And, of course, my article about the kidnapping will be in tomorrow's paper."

"I hope you know everybody who ever said hi to you in the grocery store is going to call you to see how you're doing."

Tracy chuckled. "Not everybody, but I have had a few calls from people who saw the news in the other papers. It hasn't been bad."

"I just hope you're being extra careful for now."

"I am. Anyway, give me a call tomorrow afternoon when you're ready to go." She paused. "Actually, you can come pick me up, and that way Jeff won't worry about me going out alone."

"I'm glad you have somebody who loves you that much. It's a wonderful thing."

"Yes, it is," Tracy said. "I think you need somebody like that too."

Amy immediately thought of Miles and then quickly put the thought out of her mind. "Maybe someday."

"Someday," Tracy repeated, but Amy didn't miss the insinuation in her tone.

"Anyway," she said, "I'll call you when I get out of school tomorrow, and we'll go over to the *Lucky Chance* and see what we can see."

"It's a date."

Chapter Ten

The next morning, Amy pulled into the gas station on her way to school. She had just turned the nozzle on when she spotted a familiar face at the pump next to her.

"Carol?" Amy walked over to the older woman. "Hi. How are you?"

Carol gave her a tremulous smile. "I don't know what's going on in the world anymore. I was shocked to hear that Tracy was kidnapped, and then I got home from my quilting bee yesterday afternoon and found that my house had been broken into."

"Oh, no. I'm so sorry. Are you all right?"

"I'm fine. Thank goodness I wasn't home when it happened."

"Definitely. Did they take very much?"

"I guess it could have been worse," Carol said, glancing at the rapidly changing numbers on the pump. "But I've always thought Canton was such a quiet, safe little town."

"What was taken?"

"All of my jewelry. I had some of my grandmother's pearls that were from her mother, the pearls she wore on her wedding day in 1882. I can never replace them."

Amy put a hand on her arm. "Oh, Carol, I'm so sorry."

"I had several necklaces and bracelets, some rings—all of them are gone. Things my husband gave me over the fifty-seven years we were married." Carol's eyes filled with tears. "And the thief took Everett's coin collection. It was something I was going to pass along to our great-grandson when I have one. Everett spent years on that collection, and he was so proud of it. I know—" Carol took a shaky breath. "I know they're just things, but they had so many memories that went along with them. How could someone take them and not realize they were taking little pieces of my life?"

"Have you told the police? Maybe they can recover your things."

"I did report it, but they said there's not much chance that anything will be recovered."

"At least you're all right," Amy soothed.

"But it's not the same. I don't feel safe anymore."

There was a sharp snap, and the numbers on the pump stopped changing. Carol took the nozzle from her gas tank, returned it to the pump, and then screwed her gas cap back into place.

"I told my son that I would let him sign me up for a security system," she said. "He's wanted me to get one for a long time, but I didn't think I needed it. I wish I had listened to him. The man at my insurance company said I should be grateful the thief didn't take any electronics. I suppose he's right, but those are easily replaced. Everett's things aren't."

Amy clasped Carol's hand and then lifted it to look at her wedding rings. "At least you still have these."

Carol managed a smile. "Yes. I'm thankful I had them on. They're the most important things."

There was another tell-tale snap from the nozzle in Amy's gas tank.

"You should go finish up too," Carol said. "I feel better just talking about this with you."

"You call me anytime. And get that security system, okay?"

Carol chuckled. "My son already arranged all that. They're coming day after tomorrow to install it."

"Good. I'll see you at church on Sunday."

"I'll be there."

Amy returned to her car and finished her transaction. She stopped to wave as Carol drove away and then got into her own car and buckled herself in.

"You took a long time, Mom," Jana said from the back seat. "It's getting stuffy in here."

"I'm sorry, sweetie," Amy said. She started the engine, and Jana let her window down. "Better?"

"Thank you," Jana said.

"Was that Mrs. Tomlinson from church?" Matt asked as they pulled into the street. "Is she okay?"

Amy hesitated. She knew what had happened to Tracy was unsettling for the kids. She didn't want to make them feel even less secure.

"Mrs. Tomlinson had some bad news, but she's all right. She lost some things her husband gave her when he was still alive, and it upset her."

Matt only nodded in response, but he didn't seem quite as uneasy. More than ever, Amy needed to find out what was going on with the *Lucky Chance.* Carol was right. Everything seemed out of whack right now. They would all feel better once they knew what was behind the events of the last few days. School couldn't be over soon enough today.

As Amy had hoped, Miles was glad to look after Jana and Matt.

"I'm happy to do anything I can if it'll help you and Tracy figure out what's going on," he said. "Is there anything else I can do to help?"

"Thanks for offering," Amy said, "but we'll be fine. We're just going to talk to Eve and some of the other people on the showboat. We shouldn't be too long."

Tracy was waiting when Amy pulled up in front of her house.

"How'd things go today?" she asked as she got into the car.

"Same old, same old," Amy said. "But I saw Carol Tomlinson at the gas station this morning. Somebody broke into her house yesterday afternoon."

"Oh, no. Poor Carol. Was she cleaned out?"

"They took her jewelry and her husband's coin collection. She's pretty shaken up, and I don't blame her. This is Canton, not St. Louis."

"I know," Tracy said. "It's crazy. Did she say there were any leads?"

Amy pulled away from the house and headed for the docks. "Not specifically, but I'm guessing there weren't. She said the police weren't very hopeful about recovering anything."

Tracy's mouth tightened. "I hate that. She should be able to feel safe in her own home. We all should." She took a deep breath and then shook her head. "I guess I'm still a little edgy."

"That's understandable, and it's okay. And we're going to find something, I feel sure of that. We'll get to talk to the bookkeeper, and I'm hoping Lyle will be there too. I really want to meet him, especially after what Robert told us."

Tracy nodded. "I definitely want to find out what he's been up to. I wonder how he did in Vegas. After what Robert told us about him, I can't imagine him hurting for money and not trying to make a little in the casinos."

"If he had any to take with him. He's not likely to tell us about that though."

"He might if he won big. I can picture him as the type who'd brag in a case like that."

"Maybe so," Amy said. "I guess we'll see."

They went aboard the *Lucky Chance* and asked to see Eve. She immediately invited them to her cabin for a talk.

"How are you?" she asked, looking Tracy up and down. "I still feel awful for putting you in danger. I just can't imagine how that happened. Not here. Not in Canton."

"I'm fine," Tracy said. "I hope everything went all right during last night's performance."

Eve's eyes lit up. "Oh, yes! The new girl, Zoe, is going to fit in perfectly, and the house was packed. I heard that we're sold out to the end of the run here. Isn't that great?"

"I didn't think our little extracurricular drama would hurt business at all," Tracy said. "I'm glad."

"I was a little nervous about it, so Rudy took me to lunch yesterday afternoon and calmed me down. It was lovely. The restaurant had the most delicious Mexican food. Los Nopales."

"Yum," Tracy said. "Their food is delicious."

"We know you're pretty busy," Amy added, "but we were hoping we could meet your bookkeeper. Is she feeling better now?"

Eve rolled her eyes. "She's fine. If she wasn't such a wannabe-star, I'd have thought she was faking it the past few nights, but I saw her last Friday. She was definitely sick. She's not that good an actress."

Amy laughed. "I take it you two aren't best friends."

"Not exactly," Eve said. "We get along all right, I suppose, but it's only a business relationship."

"Do you think she'd talk to us?" Tracy asked.

"I can introduce you, if you'd like," Eve said, "but my son's supposed to be here in a few minutes, so I can't do much more than that. Is that all right?"

"Sure," Amy said. "But we'd like to meet Lyle too. Has he returned from his trip?"

Eve nodded. "He came back Monday night. I think he and Danny are in his office, going over the setup for our next production."

"Does he know about what happened Sunday night?" Tracy asked.

Eve nodded again. "He was pretty hot about that. He didn't like that we let you go on stage in the first place, since you're not officially a cast member, though I think he was happy he didn't end up having to pay you for your work. I think he's worried you're going to sue him or something."

"He doesn't have to worry about that," Tracy said. "I just want some answers and to see the person who kidnapped me brought to justice."

"Maybe you should tell him that," Eve suggested. "It might make him easier to talk to."

Tracy looked at Amy. "Maybe we'd better start with the bookkeeper and let Lyle and Danny get finished with what they're working on before we interrupt."

"Okay," Eve said, pulling her robe more tightly around herself. "But I would take anything she says with a grain of salt."

"Why?" Tracy asked.

"She's a little wacky," Eve said. "Always coming up with conspiracy theories. Not that I care what she says. Come on."

She led Amy and Tracy to the end of the corridor and knocked on the last door on the left. She was answered with silence and finally knocked again.

"Are you in there, Fran?"

"I'm coming, I'm coming," said a voice from the other side of the door. "Hold on."

The door opened, revealing a young woman with sun-streaked curls and tanned skin.

"Oh," she said, her annoyed expression changing abruptly, "I didn't know you brought company."

"This is Fran Taylor," Eve said. "Fran, this is Amy Allen and her sister, Tracy Doyle."

"Tracy Doyle." Fran looked them over, and then she gestured with one heavily ringed hand. "You're the one who got taken off the boat on Sunday, right?"

Tracy nodded. "We were wondering if we could talk to you for a few minutes. If you have time."

Fran's eyes narrowed. "Talk to me about what?"

"We're trying to figure out what happened Sunday night," Amy said.

"The police were already here," Fran said, crossing her arms. "I couldn't tell them anything, because I didn't leave my cabin that night. I was sick."

"We understand that," Amy said. "We were hoping to get a little information about the boat and the people who live on it. Would you mind?"

Fran looked warily at Eve, but Eve shrugged.

"It's up to you, honey. I have to go." She gave Tracy a wink. "You're on your own."

Fran waited until Eve was out of sight before she finally smiled. "Come on in. I don't know what I can tell you, but you can ask me whatever you want. And don't worry, I'm not contagious anymore."

She stood back and let them inside. Her cabin couldn't have been more different from Eve's genteel lavender nest. It was all bright colors and chrome and white furniture with sleek, utilitarian lines. The walls were covered with posters from Broadway shows, and her multi-level desk was home to what appeared to be the latest in computers and related gadgetry.

"Wow," Amy said, looking the electronics over. "That's quite an impressive collection."

Fran grinned. "My dog, Marco, and I are big on social media."

A tiny Pomeranian lifted his head from the designer dog bed he was curled up in, and Fran hurried over to him.

"Did we wake you up?" she cooed, cuddling the dog in her arms.

Marco whimpered and sleepily struggled to get back into his bed. Fran carried him with her to the black brocade love seat and sat down, inviting her guests to take the brightly upholstered chairs on the other side of the glass-and-chrome coffee table.

"Now," she said, settling the dog in her lap, "what would you like to know?"

Amy glanced at her sister and then back at the bookkeeper. "We understand you do the accounting for the showboat. Is that just for the boat? Or does that include the theatrical company too?"

"It's everything," Fran said. "There are expenses for running the boat, for running the kitchen, and for putting on the shows. The only income is from ticket sales. Sometimes we have a river cruise with just a dinner served, so there's no production involved, but that's usually in February when Lyle gives the actors a month off. But it's not really a month off, because they have lines and blocking to learn for the next season's repertoire."

"And they still live on the boat during that time?" Tracy asked.

"Mostly," Fran said. "Some of them take real vacations or go visit family. Some of them get jobs on Broadway or in Hollywood and don't sign up for another year, but there aren't many of those. And sometimes Eve and Danny decide to let people go altogether."

"Eve does casting too?" Amy asked, surprised.

"Not officially," Fran said. "But she's definitely one of the decision-makers. If she doesn't like somebody, that person isn't going to be around long."

Amy studied her face for a moment. "Does she like you?"

Fran smirked. "We're not exactly best friends, but we get things done."

Amy wanted to ask her more, but she figured it would be better not to press too hard. Not right away, anyway. "What about the rest of the people on the *Lucky Chance*?"

"They're all right," Fran said with a shrug. "Like I told the police, I can't think of anyone who would have a reason to kidnap somebody. I can't say I haven't wondered if something weird was going on now and then."

"Something weird?" Tracy asked.

"Well, I'm not entirely sure what's going on," Fran said confidentially. "But I know Eve has been having some kind of argument with her son."

"Eve?" Tracy and Amy said at the same time.

"I don't know exactly what it was about," Fran said, "but he's come to see her several times since we've been docked here. I heard him say something about him finally being twenty-five and asking her to at least let him see a statement for 'the account.' I don't know what account, but she told him he'd have to wait."

"I wonder if it's some kind of trust or something," Tracy said.

"You told the police about this?" Amy asked. "It doesn't seem like it would be connected to what happened to Tracy."

"They asked me if anything unusual has been happening lately," Fran said as she played with the teal-colored bow on the top of Marco's head. "It's probably just a family matter, but they told me anything could be important."

"That's true," Tracy said. "Did you tell them about any other unusual things?"

Fran rolled her eyes. "There's Lyle, of course, but everybody knows about him."

"Everybody?" Amy asked, again trying not to push.

"Lyle loves a sure thing," Fran said, her smirk returning. "Only he's not very good about figuring out which ones are actually sure."

That lined up with what Robert had said about Lyle's gambling, but that wasn't illegal.

"Did you also overhear that?" Amy asked her.

"I'm the bookkeeper, remember?" Fran nodded toward the computers. "I know what comes in and what goes out."

"And you think something weird is going on with him too?" Tracy asked.

Fran picked up Marco from her lap and cuddled him under her chin. "I don't like to be involved in anybody's business, but I was a little bit worried, so I asked him about it."

"What did you ask him?" Amy asked. "Is money missing? Something wrong with the books?"

"Just more money than usual going out," Fran said. "I could tell he was hiding something, you know? He told me he was the owner of the company and any withdrawals he took were accounted for. He said he has the right to do what he thinks is best with any of the company assets. He said I could tell the police whatever I wanted and that he didn't have anything to hide. So that's what I did."

"Probably just personal matters," Amy said, not sure she believed her own words.

"We haven't met Lyle yet," Tracy said. "He was in Vegas when we were here before. Does he go there often?"

Fran shook her head. "Not since I've been here, and that's nearly three years now. I've heard he usually does his gambling in places along the docks. It's really none of my business. I should have never said anything to him. I was just worried about what would happen to all of us on the *Lucky Chance* if he got into trouble."

"That makes sense," Tracy said.

"Seems like there's already been a little bit of trouble even before the kidnapping," Amy said, thinking of Robert's confrontation with Lyle the Friday before.

"True," Fran said. "Lyle had a pretty good dustup with somebody in his office recently."

"Was that Friday?" Amy asked, surprised to have her bring up the situation she was thinking of herself.

Fran thought for a minute. "No. I was sick as a dog on Friday."

Marco yipped, and she gave him a hug.

"Not you, precious," she cooed. "You're too cute to be sick."

"When was it?" Tracy asked.

"It was Saturday morning, right before he left for Vegas."

"Could you tell what the argument was about?" Amy tried not to sound too eager. "Or who he was talking to? Was it somebody who works here?"

"No," Fran said decidedly. "I'm sure it wasn't somebody I know. Lyle called him Robert."

Chapter Eleven

*A*my gasped and looked at her sister.

"What else did he say?" Tracy asked.

"I don't know," Fran said, stroking the tiny dog. "All I could make out was Lyle telling him to get off the boat and stay off or he'd get in trouble."

"Did the man see you?" Amy asked.

"I took off when I heard the door start to open," Fran said, "but it's a long hallway. He might have seen me before I got back to my cabin. I don't know."

"Did you tell the police?" Tracy asked her.

Fran shook her head. "It had nothing to do with what happened to you."

Maybe it didn't, Amy thought, *or maybe it did.*

"I think you should consider telling the police," she said. "They'll know what applies to the case and what doesn't."

"I guess." Fran snuggled her dog closer. "We don't want anything bad to happen, do we, honey baby?"

The dog wiggled his whole body and licked her face, making her laugh.

"Is there anything else out of the ordinary you've noticed recently?" Tracy asked her.

"I guess that's all," Fran said. "None if it seems like a big deal to me though."

"Well, let us know if you think of anything else." Tracy handed her a business card and stood up. "Thanks for talking to us. Do you think Lyle has time to see us?"

"He ought to," Fran said. "Last I heard, he was in his office. I'd introduce you, but he'd probably like you better if I didn't."

Amy forced herself not to frown. "We know where his office is," she said smoothly, and she stood up too. "We'll just introduce ourselves, right, Tracy?"

"Sure," Tracy said. "Thanks again, Fran. I'm glad you're feeling better."

"Thank you," Fran said, and her dog gave a little squeak-toy bark. "Marco says come back anytime."

She walked Tracy and Amy to the door and, with a wave, shut it after them.

"What did you think of her?" Tracy asked, keeping her voice low as they walked toward Lyle's office.

"She overheard Lyle and Robert arguing," Amy said. "And Robert might have seen her and realized there was a witness to his argument with Lyle. Do you think she was the one who was meant to be kidnapped Sunday night?"

"That definitely makes me wonder if he meant to scare her into keeping her mouth shut about what she heard and then realized his men had taken the wrong person. That would explain why they let me go without asking for money."

"Exactly." Amy shook her head. "It still doesn't sound like something Robert would do. And he's not a member of the cast or crew, so how would he know the ins and outs of the play? Also, I don't understand why he'd come back the next morning. You'd think he would have said everything he wanted to when he was there Friday."

"True, but since we heard them arguing on Friday too, I don't think she's lying."

"Maybe not, but there's something going on with her. If the owner doesn't like her and the star of the show doesn't like her, why does she still have a job here?"

"I wondered the same thing," Tracy said. "And how much does a bookkeeper for a small-time operation like this make anyway?"

"Exactly. That little dog must have cost a lot of money, not to mention the technological display she had going on in there."

They walked a little farther down the carpeted corridor, and Amy glanced at the numbered doors they passed. She supposed the rooms were occupied by the people who worked on the show. Did they all know about Lyle's gambling and Eve's situation with her son? Or had Fran nosed out those things for her own purposes?

"Did you believe her?" Amy asked. "I mean about being concerned that something weird was going on?"

"I don't know. I realize it's too early to say for sure right now, but suppose Fran did find something out, either about Eve or about Lyle, and was getting paid to keep quiet about it?"

"That's what I was wondering." Amy stopped as they approached Lyle's office. "But no matter what's going on with them, what does that have to do with your kidnapping? And we still have the fact that if it was Fran they were really after, they would have known she'd been replaced."

"Eve would have known," Tracy said. "But maybe Lyle didn't. Fran said she was sick on Friday and he left on Saturday morning. So he might have assumed she'd be going on by Sunday night."

"And Eve wouldn't have any reason to kidnap you, would she?"

"She might," Tracy said reluctantly. "If she has some kind of money trouble."

Amy looked at her in disbelief.

"I'm not saying that's the case," Tracy said. "But it's a possibility."

"She was on stage the whole evening."

"That would be a good alibi, wouldn't it? Anybody could hire a couple of thugs to do a job like that."

"But nobody got any money from you," Amy said. "You and Jeff don't have that kind of money in the first place."

"Maybe she thought we did."

"But nobody even tried to get money from you."

"Not a penny."

"And she was with us the whole time anyway, from the time she found out you were gone until you called us to come pick you up. She couldn't have been involved."

"Like I said, anybody could hire somebody," Tracy said. "And Eve's a good actress. Meaning she could pretend to be worried about me and shocked to hear I'd been kidnapped and all that even if she was behind it."

"We haven't met Lyle yet, so it's a little early to be settling on one particular suspect, don't you think?"

Tracy managed a smile. "You're right. Let's go see if Lyle will tell us anything."

"Like what he and Robert were arguing about? Or if he knew Fran wasn't going to be in the play Sunday night?"

Tracy's smile widened. "We can try, can't we?"

They walked up to Lyle's office door, and Tracy knocked.

"It's open," a tenor voice said in response.

She turned the knob and pushed the door open. Behind a cluttered desk sat a man with sandy hair and a red mustache, looking at them with narrowed eyes.

"Can I help you?"

"We don't want to interrupt anything, but we were hoping you had a minute to talk to us. I'm Tracy Doyle, and this is my sister, Amy Allen."

"Oh." His wary look gone, he stood up. He was a tall man with a round belly. "Ms. Doyle, Ms. Allen, please, come in. I've been meaning to get in touch with you. What happened to you on Sunday night was terrible, and even more so because it happened here on the *Lucky Chance*. How are you? Please, have a seat."

He gestured to the two rather battered leather chairs in front of his desk, and Amy and Tracy sat down in them.

"I'm fine," Tracy assured him. "Thank you."

"I'm very happy to hear that," he said.

"I like your office," Amy said, looking around at the dark-stained oak walls and the heavy furniture that might well have been made sometime in the eighteen hundreds. "I think Mark Twain would have been comfortable here in his riverboat days."

"It does fit the style of the boat, doesn't it," Lyle said, seating himself again. "But I can't take credit for it. As far as I know, this has all been here since the *Lucky Chance* first launched." He rapped sharply on his desk. "They knew how to make furniture back then."

"Definitely," Amy said.

The desk, and the whole office itself, to be honest, was shabby. The furniture was well built and was probably the finest of its kind back when the *Lucky Chance* was the queen of the Mississippi. But it had obviously stood up to hard use over the years. Lyle seemingly wasn't the first owner who valued utility over aesthetics.

"So how can I help you?" he asked. "I hope you understand, Ms. Doyle, that since you weren't actually an employee at the time of the incident and were, in fact, in a non-public area of the boat without formal permission, LCI, that's our corporation, can't be held responsible for what happened, as sorry as we are that it happened in the first place."

He looked at Tracy anxiously, but she immediately put his fears to rest.

"I didn't come here to get money from you or your corporation. I'm only interested in finding out why I was kidnapped that night. My sister and I were hoping you might have some ideas about that."

"I'm afraid not," he said regretfully. "If I had been here at the time, you never would have been in the position to be taken in the first place. I've had some fairly stern conversations with Eve and Danny about them asking you to fill in."

"I don't think any of us could have predicted what happened on Sunday night," Tracy said.

Amy leaned forward in her chair. "They were just trying to keep from having to cancel the show that night. I think you should be proud of them for finding a quick solution. A cheap one too. Tracy didn't ask to be paid."

She thought, if nothing else, Lyle would appreciate that aspect of it.

"That's all well and good for employees," he said with a sniff, "but I have to think of things like legal liabilities, union regulations, and any number of things they don't have to answer for." He smiled. "You understand, I'm sure."

"Yes, of course," Tracy said. "But, again, I don't have any intention of suing anybody, especially not LCI."

"If it's about your grandmother's screen," Lyle said, "I would completely understand if you'd prefer to not loan it to us anymore. *Lucky Chance* really can't be responsible if something happens to it once we leave Canton. And what we were using before is certainly serviceable."

"That one didn't seem to go with the rest of the beautiful set furniture," Amy said diplomatically.

"We had another one," he said. "A nice one too, but it got broken while it was in storage before this run of the play. We had to find a quick replacement and ended up with the one we have now. It'll do. We don't have the money to buy new stuff every day, you know. Sure, we do a good business, but we have a lot of expenses too. You think it's easy to feed and house a bunch of actors besides the crew and other support people needed to put on a show? You think poached salmon and French pastry come cheap? And that doesn't include the cooks and waiters either."

Not to mention an addiction to gambling, Amy thought, but that didn't seem to have anything to do with what had happened to Tracy. It probably did have something to do with the showboat being repossessed and with his conflict with Robert though. She didn't dare ask him straight out about that.

"I suppose it's hard to keep everything going," she said.

"It's always hard," he said. "And, yeah, in lean times, people don't go out as much. There are nights we don't sell out."

"What do you do when you're running short?" Tracy asked. "I'm sure you still have bills to pay. Payroll to meet."

Lyle's eyes darted to the empty inbox on the corner of his desk, but if the repossession letter Robert claimed to have seen had once been there, it wasn't there now.

"What everybody does," he said with an uneasy laugh. "Take out a loan until things get better. Or try to hit it big at one of the casinos."

"Did you?" Amy asked. "In Vegas, I mean."

Lyle looked disgusted. "Nah. It was a total bust this time."

"I thought maybe you'd won some money," Tracy said.

"What would make you think that?" He frowned. "Sounds like somebody's been talking. I'm sure it was Fran. It was, wasn't it?"

"Why do you say that?" Amy asked him, keeping her expression neutral.

"Because that little girl has a big mouth." He laughed. "She's always worried about everybody else. Making sure the show is doing all right and she's not going to have to find another job and that kind of thing. Being young and on her own, I guess that's natural enough. But she needs to let me take care of things businesswise. I've been doing this for long enough to know what works and what doesn't. Yeah, we've had some tough times, but things are changing now. And she can tell anybody whatever she wants about how I run things. I have nothing to hide."

Now, Amy thought. *There's nothing he has to hide now. But what's changed?*

"I suppose you have squabbles with your employees or visitors from time to time," Tracy said.

Amy made sure not to look at her. Tracy's voice had the disarming tone Amy had heard her use when she conducted interviews, especially when she was trying to get her subject to open up.

"Everybody has squabbles," Lyle said. "We're like a big family here on the *Lucky Chance,* and sometimes family members rub each other the wrong way. And they get over it too. Most of the time."

"Sure," Tracy said.

"And, yeah," Lyle added, "now and again we get somebody on board who kicks up a fuss. I had somebody in here last week making all kinds of threats."

"Who was that?" Tracy asked, looking startled.

"Oh, some old geezer I used to be on the river with. He's had a grudge against me for years. Even tried to get me in trouble with the police over it, but nothing ever came of it, because there was nothing in it to start with."

Amy smiled. "We didn't come to ask you about your business anyway. We're only trying to find out about Sunday night."

"Sure." Lyle smiled too. "So, about that screen Eve borrowed from you. Are you sure you want to leave it with us? Like I said, LCI can't be liable for it."

"We understand," Tracy said. "And we agreed to loan Eve the screen only until you come back this way and return it. She said it would just be a short time."

"Fair enough," Lyle said. "As long as you understand I can't take responsibility for it, either personally or on LCI's behalf."

Tracy nodded. "I think you've made that clear."

"Then I don't know how I can help you. I was out of town all last weekend. I didn't know anything about any of this until I came on board Monday night."

"We realize that," Amy said, "but it seems clear that whoever was behind this whole thing must have been very familiar with how the play went and knew who would be where at exactly what time. We think it had to be somebody either in the cast or the crew."

"Seems logical," Lyle said. "But who? Why?"

"That's exactly what we're trying to find out," Tracy told him. "We were hoping you might have some ideas."

He shook his head. "Believe me, I've been thinking this over since I found out about it, especially after the police interviewed me. Frankly, I don't know why anybody would want to kidnap you and then let you go right after. Somebody thought better of it at the last minute? Somebody who felt sorry for you? Maybe somebody you know?"

Tracy's face was grim. "Amy and I wondered that ourselves, but that would narrow it down to just Eve."

"And she was the one who convinced you to fill in on Sunday night," Lyle said. "Man, I don't know what to say. That wouldn't be like her."

"No," Tracy said. "Not at all."

"But why?" Amy pressed. "Why would she want to in the first place?"

"That I wouldn't know," Lyle said. "An old grudge, maybe?"

"I don't think so," Tracy said. "I haven't seen her in years, and even in school we were always friends. Not best friends or anything, but we never had any problems, not even a mutual crush."

"I don't know what to tell you. I still wonder if the kidnapper was somebody you know. There are a lot of people around the docks, and I can't vouch for everybody who comes aboard the *Lucky Chance*. Not all of them come by invitation." Lyle checked his watch and then stood up. "I'm really sorry, but I'm going to have to cut this short. I have a meeting to go to."

Amy and Tracy both stood too.

"Thanks for taking the time to talk to us," Amy said.

Tracy gave him her business card. "If you happen to think of anything, even if it's only an improbable theory, please give me a call. You never know what's going to spark an idea."

"I'll do that." Lyle slid the card into his shirt pocket. "For sure."

Amy and Tracy didn't say anything until they were out on the deck and bathed in the late-afternoon sunlight.

"What do you think?" Amy asked.

"It seems like things are turning around for him financially." Tracy glanced back at the door they had just come through. "He seems pretty sure of himself now, even if he might have paid off Fran to keep quiet about something earlier. And if Robert's right, he got away with this kind of thing before, so he must be at least somewhat good at it."

"True. And I'm still wondering what's going on with Eve. She may have had nothing to do with the kidnapping, but it sounds like something is going on with her son and money. Fran said—"

Amy broke off when someone came out onto the deck behind them. She shaded her eyes for a moment and then recognized the young man. It was Eve's son, Flynn.

Just the one she wanted to talk to.

Chapter Twelve

*F*lynn," Amy said. "How are you?"

He smiled. "Hello. It's good to see you again."

"Your mother told us she was meeting you," Amy said. "How are you?"

"Eh," he said with a shrug.

"Something wrong?" Tracy asked.

"Oh, you know." He gave her a sheepish smile. "Moms. It doesn't matter if you're fifty or something, they always think they need to look out for you."

Tracy chuckled. "I have a twenty-nine-year-old and a twenty-seven-year-old, and I still have those feelings, though I've learned to keep them to myself most of the time."

"I'd understand it better if I was fifteen, but I'll be twenty-five on Sunday."

Amy remembered what Fran had said she overheard between Flynn and Eve. Was this related?

"Happy birthday," she said. "Is something special going to happen when you're twenty-five?"

Flynn nodded. "My grandmother, my dad's mom, left me some money in a trust when she died. It was a decent amount seventeen years ago, so I'm guessing, hoping really, that it's grown over time.

Dad always let me see the statements on my birthday, even after he and Mom broke up, but when he died, Mom became the trustee."

"She didn't keep you up to date on the trust?" Amy asked.

"She showed me the statements for a while," Flynn said, "but then I got out of school and on my own and she was working all over the country. We weren't always together for my birthday or together much at all, really. I didn't worry about it. I knew the money would be there when it was time, and I was happy to let it stay where it was and grow."

"But?" Tracy asked.

"She's being..." He paused, his forehead puckering. "Difficult isn't the right word. Elusive, maybe. She keeps telling me it's not my birthday yet and she wants it to be a big surprise for me. I guess that's all right, but it'd be nice to know how much to expect so I can make some plans about what I'd like to do with it."

"Maybe you could talk to your mom about what you want to do," Tracy said. "It's possible she'd be willing to give you more details about your trust if she knew what you had planned."

"No," he said. "I already know she's not going to approve."

"How do you know if you don't talk to her about it?" Amy asked.

"I just know." He raked his hand through his thick hair. "I don't know how much she's told you about me."

"Not much," Tracy said. "A little for the article I'm writing, but nothing personal about you, I promise."

"Good," he said. "I'm a graphic designer. Mom was awesome about sending me to a great school, and I've been working for a good company for the past couple of years. But I realized this isn't how I want to spend the rest of my life."

"What is it you want to do?" Tracy asked.

"I still want to be a graphic designer," he said, "but working for somebody else isn't for me. I've been talking to one of my coworkers for the past year or so, and we both want to try something on our own. Together."

Amy grinned. "That's exciting. Having your own business is a big step."

"It is," he said. "We've been doing a lot of research on how to get started—the kind of capital investment we'd need and how to handle the practical part of running the company. I think we're ready. We're just waiting on my trust fund."

"Will you still be in Kirksville?" Tracy asked.

He nodded. "Yeah. We found a house we like a lot."

"Really?" Amy said. "Not office space?"

Flynn gave her a sly grin. "We'll have office space in our house... after we get married."

"Ah," Tracy said with a laugh, "so that's the part you're not telling your mom."

"Yeah, pretty much." He looked sheepish, but there was also a spark of anticipation in his eyes. "Emily and I hit it off the minute we met. We got hired the same day at the same company, right out of college. We found out we had a lot in common, even in our design style, but we learned a lot from each other too. We just...fit."

"Why don't you tell your mom?" Tracy asked him. "I think she'd be really happy for you."

"No," he said.

"Has she met Emily?" Amy asked. "Is there a reason you think she wouldn't like her?"

"They haven't met," Flynn said. "I've told her about Em a couple of times, but as far as Mom knows, she's just a coworker. I think she'd like Em if she gave her a chance. She's amazing."

Amy couldn't help a tiny pang of longing. It was obvious he was crazy about this girl, and she was truly happy for him, for anyone who found someone to share life with.

Tracy frowned. "I guess I don't understand the holdup then."

"I think Mom means well," Flynn said earnestly, "but I don't want to stir things up when I'm so close to getting the money. I don't want to worry her over it or have her try to think of some excuse not to settle it right away."

"I think you should tell her straight out what you want to do," Tracy said. "She might surprise you and be all for it."

He shook his head. "I don't think now's the time. I know she's a little shaken up by what happened to you, and she's really involved with what Rudy Daheim's doing. You know he's talking about investing in the show, right?"

Amy and Tracy both nodded.

"Mom thinks her career will take off if that happens. He wants her to be one of his star attractions when the showboat franchise is expanded."

"Wow," Tracy said. "That'll be great. I don't know what she makes now, but I'm sure that would give her a substantial increase."

"Don't tell her I told you," Flynn said, "but her boss doesn't pay that much, even to the talent."

Amy gave Tracy a wry look. Based on what they'd found out about Lyle, that was hardly a surprise.

"I don't know how she does it," he added, "but Mom seems to make her salary go a long way. I guess she's learned to manage money better than she did when I was a kid."

"Better to learn it late than not at all," Tracy said.

"Anyway," Flynn said, "I was in there trying to get her to give me some information on the trust, but she turned me down again. She said she's just got too much on her mind to deal with it right now."

"She'd probably like to enjoy your company without having to talk finances," Amy suggested.

"Yeah, probably." He glanced toward the door again. "It's not like I've badgered her about it. We had a long lunch together yesterday, practically all afternoon, and I didn't even mention it." He sighed. "Sorry about dumping all this on you. It just kind of came out."

"It's not a problem," Tracy assured him. "Sometimes it helps to get things off your chest." She patted his arm. "I'm sure you and your mom will work it out. She might not be the most practical person in the world, but I know she means well."

"Yeah," he said. "And who knows? Maybe if the deal with Rudy and his investors goes through, she'll have enough to invest in the company Emily and I are starting."

"True," Amy said.

"Okay, well, I guess I'll see you around sometime."

Flynn waved and walked off toward the parking lot.

"That's a surprise," Tracy said when he was out of earshot.

"What?" Amy asked.

"He seems like a level-headed, practical young man. That part of him must have come straight from his dad."

"Could have. Or he could have learned to be that way out of self-preservation. Somebody in the family has to be realistic, right? But I'm a little bit confused. Didn't Eve say she and Rudy had lunch together yesterday afternoon? I'm sure she did."

"She did." Tracy glanced back toward the *Lucky Chance*. "Maybe Flynn went with them and Eve just didn't mention that part."

"I guess that's possible." Amy checked her watch. "I have to go get the kids. Miles is going to wonder where I am."

"I'm sure they're fine, but I suppose you're right. And I'd better get home too, before Jeff sends out a search party."

Once she had dropped Tracy off at home, Amy went straight to Miles's house. She found him and the kids working on a jigsaw puzzle at the dining room table.

"Pretty," Amy said, studying the nearly done picture of a herd of zebras on the Serengeti Plain.

"Pretty maddening, more like," Miles said, scowling at the puzzle piece in his hand. "All those black and white stripes. At least it's not all that big."

"I found one," Jana crowed, snapping a piece into place.

"Me too," Colton said. "We're almost done."

"You kids finish up," Miles said, standing. "Would you like some coffee, Amy?"

"That would be wonderful," she said. "I feel like I haven't had a break all day."

"Come on," he said, heading toward the kitchen. "Coffee shouldn't take long. Do you want something flavored? I have several."

"Just regular coffee," she said. "Nothing fussy. Some good, strong coffee will be perfect."

"That works." He pulled out a chair for her and then went to the coffee maker. "I have some cookies too. Store-bought."

"No thanks. Coffee is enough." She glanced toward the dining room. "I hope Jana and Matt weren't any trouble."

"Not a bit. They all get along great. And it helps that we had something fun to do."

"Smart dad," she said.

"I have to have learned something over the past few years, right?"

"I hope I get better at parenting as I go along. There's always something I wish I had handled better."

"Welcome to life," he said with an understanding smile. "And I think you're doing just fine."

"It's sure nice to know I can count on you to lend a hand when I need it."

"Anytime," he said. "You know that."

She nodded.

He poured two cups of coffee and brought them to the table.

"Did you learn anything?" he asked as he sat down.

"A couple of very interesting tidbits." She took a deep breath, letting the rich aroma of fresh coffee seep into her. "But nothing that really solves anything."

"No?"

She took a long drink and then told him about meeting Fran and Lyle and about talking with Flynn. "We definitely ended up with more questions than answers."

"I wish I had some amazing solution for you," he said once they had discussed her questions, "but I'll give all of this some thought."

"I'd appreciate that. If you come up with anything, let me know." She drained her cup and stood. "I'd better get the kids home. Thanks for watching them."

"Anytime," he said again.

He walked with her back into the dining room. Natalie was putting in the last piece of the puzzle.

"Done!" she said proudly.

"Good job," Miles said. "Good job, all of you. We enjoyed having you guys over. We're still on for Saturday, right?" he asked Amy.

"Right," she said, smiling at Natalie and Colton. "We'll see you then."

She got her kids into the car and back home and was in the middle of grading some papers when her phone rang.

"Ugh," she muttered. "Who's that?"

She was surprised when she saw Tracy's name on the screen.

"Hey," she said when she answered the phone. "What's up?"

"Not much," Tracy said. "Are you busy?"

Amy chuckled. "Supposed to be, but I think I need a break."

"Good. I just got a call from Eve. She said she and Rudy want to come over tomorrow afternoon and talk to me."

"Will Eve have time? The play's still running, isn't it?"

"That's why they have to make it in the afternoon," Tracy said. "I think he's been trying to get her to convince me to push his theatrical investments in my article on our graduating class."

"Are you going to?"

"That's what I wanted to talk to you about. What do you think I should do?"

"I don't know," Amy said. "He seems all right, I guess, but I don't know anything about this kind of thing. His website was kind of sparse, but I don't know if that's a big deal. He says he likes being able to travel around on his own making deals, so he doesn't need anything fancy."

"But I don't know if I want to promote his business for him either."

"Then you shouldn't. Maybe he only wants a mention. Eve said she'll probably do really well if he gets investments for a lot of showboats and she gets to be the prima donna of the whole enterprise."

"Maybe he wants me to do an article on him," Tracy said. "Whatever he wants, this might be the perfect opportunity to talk to both of them again."

"Especially since we didn't really have a chance to talk to Eve today. There are a couple of things Fran said that I'd like to get her opinion on. Or maybe I should say corroboration of. And Rudy's an outsider. He may have noticed something while he was on the boat that nobody else thought to mention."

"True. We got some interesting information on the showboat today. And I got some even more interesting information tonight."

"Oh, really?" Amy asked. "Tell me."

"Well, Jeff and I ended up going out for dinner. He's still in the spoiling-me stage, and Mexican food sounded good anyway, so we went to Los Nopales. The waitress there doted on me because of my article about the kidnapping. She knew I was in the play that night and that I had gone to school with Eve. And she wanted to tell me all about Eve eating lunch there the day before."

"Ooh, did the waitress say who Eve was with?"

"Yes," Tracy said. "She told me it was a young man and she was sure it was Eve's son."

Chapter Thirteen

Amy clutched her phone a little tighter. "So Rudy wasn't with Eve on Tuesday afternoon like she told us?"

"Not according to the waitress who served her at Los Nopales," Tracy said. "And I don't think there's much chance Rudy could be mistaken for Eve's son. She did say Eve was there all afternoon, so that confirms what Flynn told us earlier."

"I don't get it. Why would Eve lie about it? There's nothing particularly scandalous about having lunch with your own son."

"I don't know," Tracy said, "but maybe we can find out a little more tomorrow when she and Rudy are here."

"Is it any of our business?" Amy asked. "Maybe Rudy doesn't even know that's what Eve is telling people. I wouldn't want to embarrass her in front of him."

"Maybe you're right. Maybe Eve told us it was Rudy because it sounded more glamorous than just having lunch with her son. And maybe she didn't want to talk about the situation with Flynn, so she acted like she hadn't been with him."

"You could be right." Amy threw her pen on the stack of papers she was grading and stretched back in her chair. "Maybe it's nothing, but I think having her and Rudy over tomorrow is a good idea. I'm definitely in."

"Jeff is going to a lecture after his last class, so he'll probably be late anyway."

"Ah. And he doesn't want you there by yourself."

"No, it's not that. We're both fine with me being alone now. I'm not going to spend the rest of my life being spooked by every little noise."

"That's good," Amy said. "I'll be there. The kids can play upstairs while we talk with Eve and Rudy. What time should I come?"

"About five, I think. Eve is supposed to report for duty at six thirty, but she said Rudy already checked with Lyle and got her special permission to check in a little late if she needs to. You can stay afterward and eat with us if you want."

"Okay."

Tracy chuckled. "Speaking of dinner, are the kids still having their cooking lesson on Saturday?"

"Yeah, about five, I think. You're coming, right?"

"Oh, I wouldn't miss it. Miles is bringing his kids? Or do you want me to pick them up on my way over?"

"That's a great idea," Amy said. "I'll call Miles and tell him you'll get Natalie and Colton. I'm sure he'll appreciate it."

"All right. See you and the kids tomorrow at five."

"See you then."

Amy ended the call and then tapped Miles's number, glad nobody but she would notice the little flutter inside her when she did. There was nothing even remotely romantic about this call or about the plans for Saturday, but that fluttery feeling got stronger when he answered.

"Amy, hi."

She smiled at the smile she heard in his voice. "Hey, Miles. I'm calling about the kids coming over on Saturday."

"It's still on, isn't it? They're really excited about it."

"Yes, it's still on. But Tracy is going to come help, and she offered to come by your house and get the kids on her way over. That way you won't have to bring them over and pick them up. What do you think?"

"That works for me," he said. "I have some paperwork I need to get to, and that'd be the perfect time for it. It'll be a lot easier to concentrate on it if I'm by myself."

"I know that feeling. So Tracy will be by a little before five on Saturday."

"I'll have the kids ready. Is there anything they can bring?"

"No," she said. "I have everything here."

Amy hesitated a moment, not ready for the call to end but not sure what to say next.

"So...how've you been?" he asked before she could think of anything. "How's Tracy doing?"

"We're both all right. We're still trying to figure out what happened to her. We've come across a lot of things that don't add up yet, but we're working on it."

"I hope you two are careful. I wouldn't want anything to happen to you."

Was that "you" singular, or plural? The little flutter came back.

"We will be," she said. "I promise. And I promise we won't do any crime fighting while the kids are at my house."

He laughed. "That's good to know. And thanks for having them over. They haven't talked about much else since you invited them."

"My kids have been looking forward to it too. We're planning on having a good time and learning a lot."

"All right then. If you decide they should bring something, let me know."

"Sure thing. Talk to you soon."

She ended the call and then wondered if she should have invited him to come too. No, he already had plans for that evening. This was supposed to be about the kids, after all, and besides, she needed to focus. Eve and Rudy were coming over to Tracy's tomorrow. It should prove to be a very informative talk.

"How long do we get to stay?" Jana asked as they pulled up in front of Tracy's house the next evening.

"You and Matt are going to go up to the guest room and play while Aunt Tracy and I talk to some people about boring business stuff," Amy told her. "And then later, we'll have dinner. You like playing at Aunt Tracy's, don't you?"

"Yeah," Jana said, "but I don't have my dolls."

"There's a whole closet full of toys and some dolls up there too," Amy reminded her. "And a lot of games and other things to do."

"I want to play with the Tinker Toys," Matt said before running up to ring the doorbell.

A moment later, Tracy opened the door and gave him a huge hug while her goldendoodle, Sadie, panted and wriggled beside her. "There you are. Come in. Come on, Jana."

Jana ran up to her and got a hug for herself and then gave the dog a big kiss on the nose.

"Go on into the kitchen," Tracy said, "I just made some cookies."

Both kids dashed into the house with Sadie chasing after them.

"How's it going?" Amy asked as she and Tracy followed them.

"All right. Eve called a little while ago to confirm she and Rudy are headed this way. I was tidying up the living room."

"I'll give you a hand," Amy said.

They had just finished when the doorbell rang.

"That'll be them," Tracy said, smoothing the quilt over the back of the couch and shushing the dog.

"Okay, you two," Amy said to Matt and Jana. "Go on upstairs, and no squabbling, okay? This shouldn't take too long. Take Sadie, and stay in the guest room."

"We will," they chorused as they hurried away.

Sadie barked excitedly and followed them up the stairs.

"I'll get the door," Tracy told Amy. "If you don't mind, would you start some coffee? And set out some cookies too. They're in the cookie jar."

"Okay," Amy said. "I'll be there in a minute."

Amy put the coffee on. By the time it was ready, she had put the cookies on a plate and fixed a tray with napkins, coffee cups, and cream and sugar. She finished preparing the tray and then carried everything into the living room.

"Amy, hello," Eve said with an engaging smile. "It's good to see you again.'

Rudy stood up. "How are you, Ms. Allen?"

"I'm doing fine, thanks," Amy said, putting the tray on the coffee table. "And please, call me Amy." She picked up a cup. "Would you like some coffee? Eve?"

She poured coffee for everyone, and Tracy urged them to help themselves to cookies.

"These are delicious," Eve said after tasting one.

"My grandma Pearl's recipe," Tracy told her.

"Oh, the famous Grandma Pearl." Eve turned to Rudy. "She owned the screen we're borrowing for the play."

"This used to be her house," Tracy said. "My husband and I live here now."

Rudy took a sip of coffee. "It's a big place. Do you write your articles here, or do you have an office at your newspaper?"

"I've been working upstairs in my office lately," Tracy told him. "My husband is a history professor at Culver-Stockton College, so he's got a lot going on when school is in session. We both stay pretty busy."

"I imagine you do." Rudy helped himself to a cookie. "I understand that, with everything that's happened to you, you haven't finished your article about Eve yet."

Tracy gave him a rueful smile. "I'm afraid not."

She was about to ask Eve how the play was going when Rudy suddenly frowned, took his phone from his pocket, and swiped the screen. "I'm sorry," he said, "but I need to take this call. I'll just let myself out for a moment."

He stood and left the room, and a moment later, Amy heard the front door open and shut. It couldn't have been more than a minute or two later when he returned.

"Sorry about that," he said. "Now, where were we? Oh, yes, your writing, Tracy. I read your account of Sunday's incident in yesterday's edition. It was very well written and engaging."

"Thank you," Tracy said. "It felt a little strange to write something like that about myself."

"But that's what made it so gripping," Eve said. "I thought it was wonderful."

Tracy shrugged. "My editor liked it."

"I can see why," Rudy said. "And that's why we wanted to come talk to you about the article about Eve."

"Not just about me," Eve said, simpering a little bit. "About our graduating class."

"True," Rudy said, "but you, my dear, will be the most interesting part of it."

Amy glanced at Tracy, who responded with a slightly raised eyebrow. He was laying it on a little thick. Eve was certainly eating it up.

"Anyway," he said, "she and I talked about what you might want to include in your article, and we were hoping you could put in a little bit about the plan we have for expanding the showboat franchise."

"What did you have in mind?" Tracy asked him. "I don't want it to sound like an infomercial."

Rudy chuckled. "No, no, of course not. We just want to include a little something about what we have planned, especially as it relates to Eve here. So it would still be about her. Would that work?"

"It wouldn't be an ad, per se," Eve said, "though the story would naturally bring attention to Rudy's company. Well, to the project itself more than to his company. Isn't that all right?"

Tracy considered for a moment and then nodded. "That ought to be fine, as long as you don't expect anything inviting potential investors to visit your website."

Rudy chuckled. "Not at all. But something drumming up a little interest in the project itself, in having showboats with various types of entertainment visiting different ports along the Mississippi, would be ideal."

"I think I can do that," Tracy said. "Especially if I can talk about Eve's role in the plan. Is she going to—"

There was a thud from overhead, and everyone looked up.

"Sorry," Amy said. "My kids are playing up there."

"Do you think you should check on them?" Eve asked.

Amy listened for a few more seconds, but there was only quiet. Then she heard the faint sound of Matt's and Jana's laughter.

"I'm sure they're fine," she said. "So, Rudy, what exactly is the plan?"

They had finished their coffee and most of the cookies by the time Rudy had explained his idea. It did sound intriguing, and Eve, of course, was all in. Amy could see why Rudy was so successful. He was a good promoter and obviously enjoyed sharing his ideas with potential partners. Finally, he glanced at his watch.

"I'm sorry," he said, standing up. "I didn't mean to take up so much of your time. Eve, we should get going. You don't want them raising the curtain without Lady Frances, and I'm sure those children upstairs are getting hungry."

Amy smiled. "It's been very interesting. I hope the whole plan is a big success."

Eve stood too. "I'm sure it will be. Rudy is an expert. I think he ought to be with some large agency working with major productions."

"Oh, no," Rudy said with a smile. "I'd rather be my own boss and work at my own pace. Sure, I could make a lot more money in

New York or Los Angeles, but I wouldn't like being under that much pressure. This way I get to do what I want and help a lot of people along the way. What could be better than that?"

"No argument here," Tracy said.

"Oh, I don't know if you've heard," Amy said, "but one of your investors had a bad experience this week."

"One of my investors?" Rudy looked alarmed. "What happened?"

"It was Carol Tomlinson. Her house was robbed."

"Oh, dear." Rudy shook his head. "I'm sorry to hear that. I was supposed to meet with her on Tuesday, but she told me she had her quilting group to go to, so we put it off until tomorrow."

Eve flashed a brilliant smile. "I told you, he ended up going to lunch with me instead."

Amy glanced at Tracy. Tuesday afternoon was when Carol's house was robbed. And Tuesday afternoon was when Rudy wasn't eating lunch with Eve.

Chapter Fourteen

"Yes, the restaurant was lovely, and the food was delicious," Rudy said.

Amy kept a placid smile on her face. He sure didn't look like he was lying.

"Not being from this area," he said, "I can't remember where it was. What was the name, Eve?"

"Los Nopales," Eve supplied.

"Nice place," Tracy said. "Jeff and I were there last night."

"Yes, Los Nopales," Rudy said. "And it was excellent. Of course, the main thing was discussing specifics about what we're going to do with the showboat company."

"Not that I know much about finance," Eve said.

"Ah, but you do know the theater," Rudy reminded her. "You're quite familiar with the day-to-day workings of just the kind of operation we're planning on. Your input has been invaluable."

Eve looked away demurely. "I'm glad to be of help."

"Eve," Tracy said, a slight wariness in her voice, "I have to ask you something. I don't want to interfere in your business, but we talked to Flynn for a few minutes yesterday before we left the *Lucky Chance*."

Eve's lips trembled. "You did?"

Tracy nodded. "I know we haven't been friends for a long time, but I hope you know I would never do anything to upset you."

Eve's eyes darted toward Rudy and then back to Tracy. "I know."

"You weren't with Rudy on Tuesday afternoon, were you?" Tracy asked.

"I-I'm sure I don't—"

"No, no," Rudy said, taking Eve's hand. "I'm not going to let you cover for me anymore."

Amy tried to read his face. He certainly didn't look like a criminal suddenly exposed. Surely he had nothing to do with the robbery at Carol's house. He dealt in large investments, not in burglaries.

"I know it's awkward," he said with a rueful grin. "Think how it must feel for me. All the money I deal with, and I had to come up with some actual cash right away."

Tracy looked as startled as Amy felt. Was he confessing?

"C-cash?" Amy stammered.

"Oh, dear," Rudy said. "It's not just awkward. It's downright embarrassing. You see this?" He pushed up his sleeve, exposing his Rolex. "This was my father's. His father gave it to him when he graduated from the university back in Germany. That was in 1933, the year Rolex flew their watches over Mount Everest to prove they would keep time under extreme conditions. My father was very proud of it."

"I'm sure," Tracy said, "but what does that have to do with where you were on Tuesday?"

Rudy chuckled. "You should know by now that I'm always on the lookout for a profitable business opportunity. A friend of mine wanted to sell me some very good investment stocks, but he needed the money right away. Part of me wanted to help him out, and part of me, of course, wanted to get a good deal on the stocks, but I didn't have any ready cash that day. I could have had plenty the next morning, but that wouldn't do. He needed the money right away."

"You're always helping people," Eve said adoringly.

"I'm afraid I failed my friend that day. I wanted to do it, but all I had that would cover what he needed was this watch. I even went as far as to go down to a broker to see what I could get on it, but when I got to the place, I realized I could never sell this watch or even risk pawning it. I turned around and went back to my hotel room."

"What about your friend?" Tracy asked.

"I connected him with another friend who was eager to make the deal." Rudy snorted. "The stocks took off a day later. Made him a mint. But I'm not sorry. I didn't want to lose this watch. It's the only thing I have left that was my father's."

"Why have Eve cover for you?" Amy asked him. "There's nothing to be ashamed of in that."

"My dear," Rudy said, "how would it look for a man who deals with large investments every single day to admit to the world that he doesn't have ready cash for his own personal investments? What would my clients think? Of course, I do have my own stock portfolio, but there was no time in the situation to liquidate anything. You see my dilemma."

"I don't know that much about investing," Amy admitted, "but I do understand that you wouldn't want to sell a family heirloom like that. It's a beautiful thing."

"I think so," Rudy said. "And you mustn't blame poor Eve for covering for me. It was such an innocent thing, but I should never have asked it of her."

"I didn't think anyone would even notice," Eve said, looking appealingly at Tracy. "I'm so sorry."

"I'm glad you told us," Amy said. "We were puzzled about it."

"I know I shouldn't have told you two a fib," Eve said. "It seemed like such a little thing, I just couldn't imagine what difference it would make."

Tracy shook her head indulgently. "It was those little things that always got you into trouble in school."

"And everyone always forgave me." Eve laughed. "I promise to lead a blameless life from now on."

"I'm just glad it's all cleared up," Tracy said. "It sounds like you and Rudy make a good team. If you don't mind, Rudy, I might even include a little about you in the article."

"A mention is all right," Rudy said. "But it's supposed to be Eve's story."

"And you're part of it," Eve said, "so of course you should be included."

Rudy shook his finger at her. "A mention is plenty." He turned to Tracy. "Remember that, please."

They all stood.

"Before you go," Amy said, "I'm wondering about something I heard earlier. I was told that Lyle was arguing with somebody in his office Saturday morning. Do you know anything about that, Eve?"

There was a touch of reluctance in Eve's nod. "I don't know any actual details, because I couldn't make out many words, but it sounded pretty fierce. I know Lyle was getting ready to fly out right about then, so I thought he was just stressed over getting to the airport on time and maybe he was taking it out on Danny, as usual. But after a few seconds, I realized it wasn't that. He was telling somebody to get off the *Lucky Chance* and not come back. 'The next time you stick your nose in my business, I'll break it,' is what he said, or something pretty close to that."

Rudy's expression was grim, but he didn't say anything.

"Do you know who he was talking to?" Tracy asked.

"No. At least it wasn't somebody I knew. Lyle called him Robert."

Amy and Tracy exchanged glances. That seemed like confirmation of Fran's story.

"I didn't know what to make of it," Eve said, "but then Danny called me to work out some blocking for our next show, so I didn't hear anything else."

"And you don't know a Robert?" Tracy asked her. "Or know of one who's been around the ship?"

"I'm afraid not," Eve said. "But then again, I don't pay that much attention. Between the deckhands and the food service people and the customers we have on and off the ship, I don't know who comes and goes."

"Will you let us know if you hear anything else about him or find out who he is?" Tracy asked her. "It might be really important."

"Oh, of course," Eve said. "The minute I hear anything, I'll call you."

"Thanks," Tracy said. "Come on, I'll walk you out to the car."

"Bye," Amy said. As they left the room, she put the empty cups and crumpled napkins on the tray with the coffeepot and cookie plate and carried them into the kitchen.

Tracy joined her a few minutes later. "Thanks for helping out."

Amy looked up from the coffeepot she was rinsing. "I don't mind. You're coming to help me with the kids on Saturday, after all."

"Of course."

"Miles says his kids are looking forward to it, and I know mine are." Amy dried her hands on the dishtowel. "Speaking of mine, I guess I ought to go see what they're up to."

"Okay. I'm going to try to do a little work before dinner. Rudy and Eve gave me some good ideas for the article."

They went upstairs and found the kids watching Disney's *Pinocchio*, using Sadie as a pillow. The dog lifted her head, thumping her tail as soon as she saw Amy and Tracy.

"Mom," Matt said. "Are you done?"

"All done," Amy said. "Are you two going to be ready for dinner, or did you have too many cookies?"

"We only had one each," Matt said.

"Can't we watch the rest of the movie?" Jana begged. "It's almost time for the whale."

Amy chuckled. "I'm sure you have time for the whale. Aunt Tracy needs to do some work before Uncle Jeff gets home."

"We thought maybe she was already working," Matt said, getting up.

"What do you mean?" Tracy asked him.

"We heard you in your office," he said. "A little while ago."

Tracy frowned. "I wasn't in my office."

"What about that thump we heard?" Amy reminded her. "Did you kids hear a thump?"

Matt and Jana both nodded.

"We thought it was Aunt Tracy or you," Matt said, his eyes darting toward the office.

"Maybe something fell over," Amy suggested, not at all convinced. "Maybe Sadie was in there."

"She was asleep most of the time," Matt said. "She looked up and growled when we heard the noise, but we told her it was okay and to go back to sleep."

"She never has been much of a watchdog," Tracy said. "Come here, Sadie."

The dog came to her, panting eagerly, tail wagging.

"Was somebody in the office, girl?"

Sadie barked and gave her a big doggy smile.

"Come on," Tracy said. "Come with me."

They all followed her and Sadie to Tracy's office. The room was quiet. A rectangle of light from the window shone across the cluttered desk.

"Go look, Sadie," Tracy urged.

The dog walked into the office, unconcerned.

"I guess nobody's here," Amy said, relieved.

"Nobody here now," Tracy said. "But what made that thump?"

There was nothing on the floor. Besides the chaos on Tracy's desk, nothing seemed out of place.

"I don't know what that was," Tracy said. "Anyway, I guess I'd better get to work while I can. Jeff should be home before long."

"Okay," Amy said. "Come on, kids. Let's go see what happens to that whale."

"Give me a few minutes," Tracy said, "and then you kids can help me with dinner. It'll be good practice for Saturday, right?"

The kids nodded eagerly, and the three of them shared a grin.

"Between you two and Natalie and Colton, we'll make a great—" Tracy stopped, her eyes fixed on her desk.

"What is it?" Amy asked. "I don't see anything."

"It's not what's there," Tracy said. "It's what isn't. My yearbook is gone."

Chapter Fifteen

"Are you sure?" Amy asked.

Tracy searched through the books and papers on her desk and then looked under it. There was no sign of the yearbook.

"I had it right before you got here," she said. "I was working on the part of the article about the Hernandez twins." She put her hand on one corner of the desk. "It was right here. I'm sure of it."

"Where could it have gone?" Amy asked, looking around. "Could you have moved it without thinking? Maybe carried it into another room when you went out? Or maybe you took it downstairs with you?"

"No, I'm sure I didn't," Tracy said. "Why would I? I knew I would have to work on the story tonight. If I was going to put it somewhere else, I would have put it back in my closet where I usually keep it."

"Did somebody come in and take it?" Matt asked, moving a little closer to Amy.

Amy put her arm around him. "We don't know yet. Maybe you'd better go check your closet, Tracy, just to be sure."

Tracy hurried out of the room. She was back less than a minute later, shaking her head.

"I'm sure I left it on the desk. I had it open to the page Chris Marks signed. He wrote, 'Off Broadway but not for long!' by his picture, and I wanted to take a photo of the autograph to head up his section of the article. I wanted to do that for each of my subjects, but now I can't."

"You can find another copy at the high school or the historical society," Amy suggested. "And Eve has hers."

"Probably," Tracy said, "but that doesn't actually help in this instance. I need the autographs that were in my book. They're a big part of the article."

Jana slipped her hand into Amy's, her brown eyes wide. "Do you think somebody's still here?"

Tracy gave Amy a look, clearly wondering the same thing. Amy didn't blame her.

"We'd better call the police," Amy said, squeezing Jana's hand. "They can check the house and make sure we're all right."

"And nobody touch anything until after they've been here," Tracy said. "We'd better go outside to wait for them."

"Good idea," Amy said. If an intruder was lurking somewhere in the house, they'd all be safer outside.

She led the kids down the stairs and picked up her purse on the way out of the house.

Tracy grabbed her phone and followed them. Once she had reported the break-in and theft, she texted Jeff.

"I don't want to interrupt his lecture, but I want him to know what's going on. He can decide whether or not to come home right away," she said to Amy.

"You know he will," Amy said, looking down toward the end of the street, hoping to see the comforting sight of a patrol car coming their way. "Especially after what happened to you on Sunday."

"I told him everybody was fine and that nothing else was disturbed, so maybe he won't be too worried."

Amy lifted one eyebrow.

"All right, all right," Tracy said. "He'll be worried, but at least he can't say I didn't tell him about it when it happened."

A few seconds later, Tracy's phone dinged. She looked at it and smiled. "He's on his way home. I hate that he'll miss the rest of the lecture, but I'm glad he's coming."

Amy was quiet for a moment. The theft of the yearbook put a whole new spin on why Tracy might have been kidnapped.

"Matt," she said cheerfully, "you and Jana see if you can tell when the police car is coming."

"Sure," Matt said, and he and Jana ran with Sadie down to the sidewalk to watch.

"Now I'm wondering if the kidnappers meant to get me after all," Tracy said, keeping her voice low.

"I thought the same thing," Amy murmured. "There has to be a connection. Obviously, somebody doesn't want you publishing that article."

"Eve's the only one who's going to be in the article who knows about it at this point, and why would she care? She's excited about the publicity for the show and about there being potential investors for the expansion Rudy's talking about. I mean, the two of them were just here giving me information to add to my story. Why would either of them want to sabotage it?"

Amy frowned. It certainly didn't make sense. "Okay, maybe it's somebody trying to sabotage *her*. Somebody jealous of her success. Somebody who wants to get back at her for something?"

"Fran," Tracy said. "She and Eve don't get along. If she was blackmailing Eve and Eve cut her off, this might be a way, petty as it is, of getting revenge on her."

"It's possible," Amy said, "but would Fran risk getting arrested for breaking and entering as well as burglary just for that?"

"I don't know. Especially if Eve could hit back with a blackmail charge."

"True. Still, we need to see if we can find out where Fran was tonight and if she knew Rudy and Eve would be here. If she knew you had company, she might have thought it was the perfect time to let herself in."

"But how would she have known where the yearbook was?" Tracy asked. "Whoever it was seems to have gone right to it."

"I don't know. I'm just trying to think of who might have taken it. How do you think the thief got in in the first place?"

Tracy winced. "I'm afraid that might be my fault. It was getting a little stuffy up there this afternoon, so I opened the window while I was working on my article. I closed it before I went down to make cookies, but I can't say I locked it." She exhaled. "Jeff is not going to be happy."

"I didn't do more than glance at the window area, but it didn't look to me like anything was broken. We probably should have checked all the upstairs windows and the ones at the back of the house."

"No, we should have done just what we did and gotten out. The police can check the windows when they get here."

Amy nodded. "You're right. I'm glad whoever it was didn't end up where the kids were playing. They're spooked enough as it is."

"I can understand that," Tracy murmured.

"We're going to figure this out, okay?" Amy clasped her shoulder.

"Yeah, okay."

"Mom," Matt called from the sidewalk, "I think that's a police car."

A few seconds later, Dale Leewright pulled up in front of Tracy's house and got out of his car. "I understand you had a break-in."

"We did," Tracy said. "About an hour ago."

"We came out here because we weren't sure if somebody was still in the house," Amy said.

"I'll check it out," Dale said. "All of you stay out here for now." He gave Jana a wink. "You too, sweetie."

She nodded solemnly.

Dale went cautiously into the house and shut the door behind himself.

A few minutes later, Jeff drove up to the house, parked his car, and hurried over to Tracy.

"Are you sure you're all right?" He put his arms around her. "Tell me what happened."

Tracy hugged him back. "Yes, I'm all right. Dale is in there, making sure whoever it was isn't hiding someplace inside. All I know is that somebody took my yearbook, the one I was basing my story on."

"As long as you're all right," Jeff said. "When was this? Did you realize it was missing when you got home from being out somewhere?"

"That's what's so unnerving about it," Tracy said. "I was home. I haven't gone anywhere all day."

"But—"

"It's all clear," Dale said as he came down the sidewalk. "I shut the door to your office. I want you to keep it closed until I can get somebody over here to dust for prints and see what other evidence might have been left behind."

Tracy frowned. "My work is in there. Can I at least go in and get it?"

"That's up to you," Dale told her. "We can't force you to let us secure the scene, but you going in there cuts down the possibility of us finding out who was up there."

"Okay." Tracy sighed. "I'll leave that door closed."

"It's not like your story is breaking news," Amy soothed. "It'll still be good no matter when it gets published."

"Yeah," Tracy said. "I know."

"Why don't we go inside," Dale suggested, "and you can tell me what happened."

"Yeah, I'd like to know too," Jeff said.

They all went into the living room. Amy settled Matt and Jana in front of the TV and resumed their movie. She didn't want them upstairs alone right now.

"I found signs that someone came in through your office window after climbing that big tree you have in back," Dale said. "I'm assuming the window wasn't locked in the first place."

"No," Tracy said. "I had it open earlier, and I guess I didn't lock it when I closed it again."

"We don't usually worry too much about the upstairs windows," Jeff said. "But we've been keeping everything locked up tight since Tracy's kidnapping."

"It probably wouldn't have made much difference," Dale said. "If the thief really meant to get in, he would have brought something to break a pane of glass and opened the window himself. This way you save the cost of having it replaced."

"That's not all that comforting," Tracy said.

"Sorry," Dale said. "Now, why don't you tell me what happened."

Tracy nodded. "Amy and I were in the living room talking with Eve Sendry and Rudy Daheim from the showboat about some things they wanted included in the article I'm writing. The kids were upstairs watching a movie. Around six o'clock we heard a thud from the room above this one. Not really loud, but a noticeable thud. We listened and heard the kids laughing, so we figured they were roughhousing a little bit."

Dale turned to Matt and Jana. "Did you hear a thud while you were watching your movie?"

Matt nodded. "We thought it was Aunt Tracy getting something out of her office," he said.

"Did either of you hear anything else?" Dale asked.

Matt and Jana shook their heads.

"Nobody said anything?" Dale pressed.

"Nothing," Jana said.

"How many people do you think it was?" Dale asked. "Just one?"

"Just one," Matt said.

"Okay," Dale said. "That's very helpful."

"Are you going to catch him?" Matt asked.

"We're going to do everything we can," Dale assured him. "Every little bit of information we can get helps us find whoever it was."

The kids went back to their movie, and Dale turned to Tracy again.

"I need you and Amy to tell me everything you remember," he said.

Between the two of them, they brought him up to date on Eve and Rudy's visit and what they'd talked about. Then Tracy told him what they had been thinking about Fran and why she might be the one who took the yearbook.

"And what if she's connected to my kidnapping?" she said suddenly.

Amy looked at her, startled. "What?"

"Think about it," Tracy said. "Who would know the exact right moment to grab me better than someone who'd played that part already?"

"I thought she was a bookkeeper," Dale said, taking notes.

"She is," Tracy said. "But she was also the understudy for that same role. She's been playing Cousin Muriel for several weeks now."

"Oh, I hadn't thought of that," Amy said. "That makes her look even more suspicious."

"I thought she was sick," Jeff said, frowning. "That's why Tracy had to fill in in the first place. Are you saying she faked it?"

Tracy crossed her arms. "She was a good enough actress to do a small stage part. I don't know why she couldn't fake being sick for a few days."

"Besides that," Amy said, "she didn't have to do the actual kidnapping. She just had to hire a couple of guys for the job."

"And her motive?" Dale asked.

"That's, uh, not as clear." Tracy glanced at Amy. "We talked to her for a little while, and we think there might be bad blood between her and Eve."

She told him about their conversation with Fran and the questions it brought to mind, especially about whether she had something she was holding over Eve, and Lyle too.

"That's not all," Amy said. "Fran said she heard Lyle having a pretty intense argument with someone in his office Saturday morning. She didn't see who it was, but it was a man named Robert. Eve told us the same thing tonight."

Dale raised his eyebrows.

"Yeah," Amy said. "And Lyle mentioned having a squabble with 'some old geezer' but didn't mention any names. Of course, the easiest explanation is that it has nothing to do with the kidnapping at all and is a private argument between the two of them." Amy hadn't forgotten Robert's explanation about the riverboat captain Lyle had framed, but that didn't explain why Tracy had ended up in Robert's boathouse Sunday night. "I didn't want to come right out and ask Lyle about it, but maybe you can."

"I'll definitely be talking to him again, and to Robert West too," Dale said. "And we've been checking around the docks for whoever might have been hired for the kidnapping. Our informants have come up with a couple of possibilities but nothing definite so far."

"That's good to hear," Jeff said. "What do we need to do now?"

"We'll take it from here," Dale told him. "Keep your doors and windows locked. You might want to cut some of the branches off the tree behind your house. Looks like that's what let your thief in and out so easily. But wait till we get a chance to look it over before you do anything. The perp might have left some evidence behind."

"I'll definitely do that," Jeff said. "I've been meaning to for a while anyway, so they don't damage the house."

"Good deal." Dale closed his notebook and then he opened it again. "I meant to tell you we found the lifeboat that we believe was used to take you from the showboat."

"Really?" Tracy said. "Where?"

"It ran aground about fifteen miles downstream. Evidently whoever 'borrowed' it just set it adrift when they were through with it."

"You're sure it's the same one?" Amy asked.

"It had *Lucky Chance* on the prow," Dale told her. "Forensics didn't find anything helpful on it. It was wiped clean before it was set loose."

"That's not much help then," Amy said.

Dale put his notebook into his shirt pocket. "I'll let you know when we have anything significant to report. Until then, be careful."

"We will," Tracy said.

"Thanks for coming over," Amy added.

Dale gave her a wink. "That's why I make the big bucks."

He got into the squad car and, with a wave, drove away.

"It sounds like you two have uncovered a lot more information since you caught me up last night, Tracy," Jeff said, "but it doesn't seem to have made anything clearer. I have to admit, I'm surprised about Robert West. I wasn't sure if this Fran was telling the truth about what she heard, but it seems like your friend confirmed it."

"It does," Tracy said. "That doesn't mean Robert had anything to do with the kidnapping though. I'm looking at Fran now more than him or anyone else. How would Robert know exactly when to have me kidnapped? Or that they'd need to get Calvin out of the way because he was the one who was supposed to kidnap my character in the play? Fran would have known those things."

"But they took you to Robert's boathouse," Jeff said. "That's quite a coincidence if he's not in on it."

Amy shook her head. "I don't know what to think anymore. Maybe someone's trying to make Robert look bad because he has a history with Lyle."

Tracy sighed. "I think we ought to get started on dinner. Matt, Jana, let's pause the movie and go figure out what to have."

"Okay." Matt pushed the button on the remote, and he and Jana jumped up. "All ready."

Between the five of them, they wrangled up a quick meal and spent the time afterward trying to make sense of the evidence they had so far. Finally, it was time for Amy to get her kids back home.

"Tomorrow's a school day," she said. Matt groaned, and Jana cheered.

"Thank you for helping me, Matt," Tracy said, putting her arm around his shoulders. She gave Jana a hug with her other arm. "And you, honey. You both get a good night's sleep, and if I don't see you before then, I'll definitely see you Saturday."

Matt broke into a big smile at that, and Jana giggled.

"Bye Aunt Tracy and Uncle Jeff," she said, hugging them both.

"Bye," Matt said.

Amy hugged her sister. "Stay safe, okay?"

"Definitely," Tracy said. "I'll call you after school. I have a lot to think about tonight."

"Make sure you get some sleep," Amy said sternly.

Tracy chuckled. "Yeah, I will. Good night."

She and Jeff walked Amy and the kids out to the car and then stayed on the driveway until Amy couldn't see them anymore.

Keep them safe, she prayed silently. *And help us find out what's going on.*

Chapter Sixteen

The next day was Friday, and by the end of the school day, Amy was really looking forward to the weekend. It was a relief when it was time for the three of them to head home. But before she had done more than get the kids settled in the car, her phone rang.

"Tracy, what's up?"

"I heard from Dale about the break-in at my house. They didn't find any incriminating evidence at all."

"That's too bad," Amy said.

"I was wondering if you wanted to go to PJ's with me and have a snack or something."

Amy's ears immediately perked up. PJ's was where Robert West hung out sometimes. "Anything specific going on there?"

"I've been thinking about Fran and whether or not we're on the right track that she had something to do with the kidnapping. What if she said what she did about Robert and had those men take me to his boathouse as a way to deflect suspicion from herself?"

Amy frowned. "I've been thinking about it too, and I'm not so sure we are on the right track. If Fran's motive was to make Eve look bad, how does kidnapping you accomplish that? And why would Eve confirm her story about hearing Robert and Lyle arguing?"

Tracy huffed. "Okay, you're probably right, but it really bothers me that Robert is implicated in this at all. I'd like to clear him if I can, at least of the kidnapping."

"The easiest explanation is that they argued both times about what happened between him and Lyle years ago, but that—" Amy stopped short. "What if we've got this backward? What if it's Lyle trying to make Robert look bad to get him off his tail? Robert's pretty up front about wanting to keep Lyle from swindling anybody else."

"I hadn't thought about that. We need to see if Dale has considered that. But I'd like to talk to Robert about all this again. I'm sure he's been trying to figure out what happened too, especially since the kidnappers used his boathouse. Do you have time to go with me to PJ's and see if he's around?"

"Yeah, but I hate to drop off the kids at Robin's or Miles's again."

"Bring them with you," Tracy said. "We can get them some kind of snack while we talk to Robert. What do you think?"

Amy grinned. "Hey, kids, do you want to meet Aunt Tracy at PJ's?"

"Sure," Matt said, and Jana nodded vigorously, her brown pigtails bouncing.

"Okay," Amy said. "Looks like we're on. Are you ready to go now?"

"I've been waiting for you to get off school," Tracy said. "See you in a minute."

"We're in luck," Amy said as she, Tracy, and the kids walked into PJ's.

Robert was sitting at a table with two men Amy didn't recognize. They looked to be in their late thirties or early forties. Dockworkers, if Amy had to guess. One of them wore a navy blue cap.

Fortunately, the table next to them was empty, so Tracy asked the waitress to put them there. Once the kids were seated and had ordered their ice cream, Amy and Tracy went over to Robert's table.

Robert smiled when he saw them. "I saw you come in. These are a couple of friends of mine, Granger and Fleet. Boys, this is Tracy and her sister, Amy. I knew their grandmother way back when."

The two men nodded politely.

"We don't want to interrupt you," Amy said, "but when you have a minute, Robert, we'd like to talk to you."

"Have a seat," Robert said. "You can talk in front of my mates, and you might be interested in what they have to say too."

Intrigued, Amy sat down across from Robert. Tracy took a seat beside her.

"I suppose you want to talk to me again about what happened on the *Lucky Chance*," Robert said.

"Yes," Tracy said.

She glanced at the two other men and then back at Robert, who encouraged her with a grave nod to go on.

"A couple of people on the showboat mentioned somebody arguing with Lyle," she said. "They said it was you."

Robert gave her a sour look. "You know that already. You heard that yourself, and I already told you what it was about."

"No," Tracy said. "This was a different time. We talked to you about Friday night. What these other people heard was the next morning. Saturday."

"Then it's a lie," Robert said disdainfully. "That's Pinson trying to make me look bad again. He was probably arguing with himself just so somebody'd hear it."

"You weren't there on Saturday morning?" Amy asked, finding it hard to believe that Lyle would put on a display like that hoping someone would overhear.

"I was not," Robert said. "My wife and I drove to Springfield to borrow a camper from her brother-in-law so our grandson, Lin, could use it. We left at seven and didn't return till around two o'clock. Anybody saying I was on Pinson's boat Saturday morning is a bald-faced liar."

Tracy frowned at him. "You must have driven awfully fast to get to Springfield and back in seven hours. I thought it was more than four hours each way."

Robert chuckled. "Not Missouri. Illinois. It's only about five hours round trip from here. And if you want to check up on me, just ask my wife or her brother-in-law. His name's Theo Glossup, and he lives at 5201—"

"No, no," Tracy said quickly.

"Or you can talk to Lin," Robert said. "He's tidying up the camper to go fishing with a couple of his buddies tomorrow. If you want, you can come by my house today and have a look at it. Ask my neighbors if it was there before Saturday afternoon."

"We believe you," Amy said, "but the people we talked to were really sure the person Lyle argued with was named Robert."

"I guess he'll do about anything to keep me from spoiling whatever it is he's got going on right now," Robert said. "And you can believe that whatever it is, it's shady."

"Either the name was a huge coincidence, or Lyle really is trying to make you look bad," Tracy said.

"Or your two witnesses are liars," Robert added with a curl of his lip.

Amy wondered again about Eve and Fran. They'd both heard the same thing Saturday morning...or had they only agreed to say so?

"We'll keep investigating," she said. "Sorry we were misled about you, Robert."

"No, it's understandable," Robert said, his expression softening. "You two wouldn't be worth your salt as gumshoes if you didn't check out whatever leads you got. But now it's my turn." There was a sudden sparkle in his eyes. "My mates here were telling me something you'd be interested to know. Tell the ladies, Granger."

Granger was the one with the hat. "We were just telling Captain Robert what we heard last night."

The other one, Fleet, leaned over the table. "Robert asked us a few days ago to keep our ears open around the docks. We were, uh, having a little game of cards Tuesday night, pretty much the same crew as usual, and O'Shea comes in with a wad of cash. We knew he was flat busted a few days before, because he wanted somebody to give him a stake to get in the game."

"Yeah," Granger said. "He was pretty hot about not getting any takers that night, but this time he was ready to play. One of the boys asked him if his grandma died or something, and he said he and Montez did a job for somebody that paid good. He's been known to do work nobody else on the dock'll touch."

"After that, though," Fleet said, "neither one of them would say anything about it." He grinned. "And they both got cleaned out anyway."

Tracy looked puzzled. "Are you saying they had something to do with Sunday night?"

"We're saying they might have," Robert told her. "I know O'Shea and Montez. They won't get paid until the fifteenth, and they were both stone-cold broke after they got paid the end of last month."

"But they could have gotten any kind of side job, couldn't they?" Amy asked.

"They could," Fleet said, "but usually any jobs around the dock that O'Shea and Montez would have known about all of us would have known about too. And I've known O'Shea a good long while. If he'd landed a plum job that the rest of us missed out on, he'd have been crowing about it from here to the coast."

"But he didn't say anything," Granger added. "Not to us."

Was there a connection here to Tracy's kidnapping? "He's not likely to tell you anything if you ask him, is he?" Tracy asked.

"Not likely at all," Robert said. "But here's what we're thinking. Fleet here just told me O'Shea is supposed to meet a woman here." He checked his watch. "In about twenty minutes. If we see him, we can call him over to the table and get him to talk a little."

Tracy's mouth turned up on one side. "And I can see if I recognize his voice."

"Exactly," Robert said. "What do you think?"

Amy looked at her sister in alarm. "But won't he recognize you?"

"I can keep my back to him," Tracy said, sounding more and more excited. "I'm sure he won't be expecting to see me here, and I don't have to see him, just hear him."

Robert nodded. "She can sit at the table with the kids and face the other way. Then we can have O'Shea sit where you are now. He'll have his back to you too. I doubt he'd even think of looking your way."

"Yeah," Fleet said, grinning. "If he's waiting for a woman, likely he'll have his eye on the door the whole time."

"Okay," Amy said finally. "It might just work. But that doesn't necessarily mean this is the guy."

"At this point," Tracy said, "I'll take any possible lead we can follow."

"Good girl," Robert said, clearly delighted. "I knew Pearl's granddaughter would be spunky. Now, sit down at that table and don't look around. Drink some coffee or eat something, whatever, and keep facing that way."

"Got it," Tracy said.

"The man's name is O'Shea," Robert said. "We'll make sure and call him that so you'll know to listen especially hard."

"And I'll keep my eye on him," Amy said. "Subtly."

Tracy sat with her back to Robert's table, but then she turned around again. "Even if I recognize his voice, that doesn't mean he's going to suddenly confess and tell you who hired him."

"Don't be too sure of that," Robert said. "If you recognize him, we'll keep him talking, and you can go call the police. If you say he's the man who kidnapped you, they'll take him in for questioning. A night or two in jail and a tempting plea offer from the district attorney has opened many a man's mouth."

Tracy grinned.

"Now let's get ready," Robert said. "If he's meeting somebody, he might come early, and we don't want him to see us talking."

Tracy reluctantly turned around.

"I'll keep watch," Amy promised her. She took the chair beside Jana. "You just keep your ears open."

"Is somebody coming to eat with us?" Jana asked, her spoon hovering between her dish and her mouth. Matt looked at them expectantly too.

Amy leaned a little closer to them. "I need you to listen to me really closely, okay?"

They both nodded.

"We have to look like we're not paying attention to anything in here but us," Amy said, "but we have to be a little bit quiet too, so Aunt Tracy can listen to what Captain Robert is talking about. I know that sounds confusing, but it's really important."

"We can do that," Matt said. "Do you want us not to talk?"

"You can talk," Amy told him. "The point is to act natural, so don't talk loudly, and don't talk softly. Be normal. And don't look over at that table, all right? Just eat your ice cream and talk to me."

"But why?" Jana asked, her forehead wrinkled.

"I can't tell you that right now," Amy said, "but I will as soon as I can. This is really, really important, so can you remember what do to?"

"I will," Jana said. "I won't be too quiet."

"Or too loud," Matt reminded her.

She scowled at him. "I know."

Amy fought a smile. "Be nice. And remember what I told you." She checked the time. "It won't be very long now."

Tracy tensed but didn't turn around. "Robert?"

"Yes?"

"You'll tell me when you see him, right?"

"I will," Robert assured her. "You make sure you don't look this way."

Matt and Jana sat staring at Amy, and she finally shook her head.

"Eat your ice cream. Don't sit there looking like there's a snake under the table."

The kids giggled and relaxed a little.

"Tell me how school was," Amy suggested. "I know we talked about it a little in the car, but I'm sure there's more. Matt, how was your math test?"

They were chatting away, not too quiet and not too loud, when the bell over the café door jingled. Robert had been talking to Granger and Fleet, and he didn't look away from them.

"Here he is."

Tracy bit her lip and looked down at the coffee she had ordered, obviously on high alert.

"Hey, O'Shea!" Robert called a few seconds later. "What are you doing here?"

O'Shea came over to his table. He was a tall, burly man with a heavy black beard. He would certainly be able to manhandle someone if he wanted to.

"I'm surprised to see the three of you," he said, his voice as rough as he looked. "I thought they poisoned all the dock rats."

The three men at the table chuckled.

"Sit down," Robert said, pushing a chair out with his foot. "Granger and Fleet are talking about getting a game together tonight. Are you joining them?"

O'Shea growled low in his throat. "I'm tapped out again. If I didn't think those two were too dumb to manage it, I'd swear they were dealing from the bottom of the deck."

Amy was afraid those might be fighting words, but Granger and Fleet only jeered at him.

"Keep playing with us, O'Shea," Fleet said. "We can always use the cash."

Amy watched her sister's face while the four men squabbled back and forth, boisterous but evidently not with any actual malice. She had to shake her head subtly at Matt and Jana because both of them sat frozen in place. After a few more seconds, Tracy pressed her lips together and nodded slightly.

O'Shea must be the one.

Chapter Seventeen

"I'll be right back," Tracy said, her voice low and conversational, and she took her purse with her as she left the table.

Amy looked over at Robert's table. The man definitely sounded like the rough type. Would he kidnap someone for money? From the look that had been on Tracy's face, Amy was sure she'd recognized O'Shea's voice.

Tracy returned to the table a short while later and gave Amy a satisfied nod. About five minutes after that, a squad car pulled up in front of the diner and Dale got out.

O'Shea glanced toward the door and then pushed his chair back. "I'd better see where Molly's got to. She should have been here already."

Before he could actually stand up, Dale came into the café and walked over to him.

"You O'Shea?"

"Who wants to know?" O'Shea snarled.

"I imagine the DA will, eventually."

O'Shea snorted and started to get up, but Dale moved closer to him. "I need to ask you a few questions, and I've got all day."

O'Shea scowled at him and then rubbed his chin. "Okay, but make it quick. I'm meeting somebody."

"Do you really want to do this in front of your friends?" Dale asked him.

"I don't know what this is about. What exactly do you want?"

Dale pulled a chair from another table over and sat down. "I'd like to know where you and your buddy Montez were on Sunday night."

"Sunday?" O'Shea snorted. "How would I know? Probably out having a drink or something. Why?"

"Were you and Montez together?"

O'Shea shrugged. "I think so. I don't always remember one particular night over another. What's going on?"

"What do you know about the *Lucky Chance*?" Dale asked him.

"I know where she's berthed. Why?"

"I'm sure there's word around about what happened there Sunday night."

O'Shea shrugged again. "Yeah. So?"

"I'd like to hear what you know about that."

"Just what I've heard around the docks. Some woman was taken off the boat and then let go. Sounds like a publicity stunt for the show they were putting on there, if you ask me. Bunch of foolishness."

Dale pushed his sunglasses up on top of his head, fixing O'Shea with a steady gaze. "And what was your part in that?"

O'Shea froze and then barked out a laugh. "I told you everything I know about it."

"You haven't told me where you were that night."

"Out somewhere. I don't remember. Montez and I hang out a lot of places. We might have run into some buddies we know. I can't remember that night in particular. I'm sure we had more than our share to drink."

"What about somebody who'd remember you?" Dale asked him, his expression unchanging.

"I tell you, I don't know. And I don't have to answer any questions I don't want to. You got nothin' on me."

"We'll see what Mr. Montez has to say." Dale stood up and pushed his glasses back onto his nose. "Let's go."

"Are you arresting me?" O'Shea stood too.

"Not unless you give me trouble," Dale said coolly. "You can come voluntarily, or I can arrest you. You get to decide."

"I want to talk to Montez."

"He's getting his own personal invite to the station. You and he can talk later." Dale took O'Shea by the arm. "Come on."

Amy held her breath when O'Shea didn't move, afraid things were going to get ugly, but then O'Shea said, "I want a lawyer."

"We'll get you one at the station," Dale said.

O'Shea addressed the other men at the table. "I was supposed to meet Molly Trent in here. Do me a favor and tell her I'll be in touch."

"Sure," Granger said.

Robert watched as O'Shea and Dale went out the front door and got into the squad car. Then he turned to Tracy.

"What'd you tell the police?"

"Just that I recognized O'Shea's voice from when I was taken. I'm sure he's the one who told me to keep quiet or he'd shoot me." Tracy shuddered. "I'll never forget those exact words or that voice."

Amy squeezed her hand. "The police will find out who he was working for."

"I'll feel better when they do," Tracy said, and then she turned to Robert. "I hope this is the end of it. I'm ready for it to be over. Thanks for telling us what you found out." She nodded at the other two men. "Thanks to all of you."

"It's no problem," Fleet said with a grin. "The docks can be a rough place, but guys like that make us all look bad."

"Is that man going to jail, Mom?" Matt asked.

"He might be," Amy said. "The police have to find out more, but we're pretty sure he's one of the men who took Aunt Tracy off the boat."

Jana scowled at the door O'Shea had gone through. "I hope they make him stay in jail a long time."

"The most important thing," Tracy said, "is that he tells the police who hired him and why."

"It's a start," Robert said. "And I'm hoping what he has to say is going to clear my name too."

"I'm still puzzled about what Eve and Fran overheard," Amy said. "About you and Lyle arguing in his office."

"I'd sure like to know about that too," Robert said. "I just flat wasn't there. Not on Saturday morning, for sure."

"I want to find out about that." Amy looked at her sister. "I think we ought to go talk to Eve again when we get a chance."

"We can try," Tracy said. "We ought to see if we can talk to Fran too. I'd like to know where she was when my yearbook was stolen."

"We'll do that. Right now, I need to get groceries for tomorrow's cooking lesson."

"And I need to get going too," Tracy said. "Jeff's taking me to see a movie. He promised me all the popcorn I can eat."

Amy chuckled. "He's sure been spoiling you lately."

"He sure has." Tracy beamed at her. "And Sunday after church he's taking me to Wayland for the afternoon."

"What are you going to do up there?"

"There's supposed to be a stock show a little ways north of the town. Nothing big, but Jeff says they'll have livestock and produce and crafts and antiques, and I don't know what all."

"I didn't know he was interested in that kind of thing," Amy said.

"Oh, not in particular. He just thought it would be a fun way to spend the afternoon together. I told him months ago that I'd like to have an Amish quilt, but I don't want to get it from a dealer. I'd rather get it directly from the maker if I can, and Jeff says there ought to be at least some Amish crafts for sale up there."

"That sounds like a lot of fun. I'll have to take the kids sometime."

Tracy started to say something, but Amy stopped her with an upraised hand.

"Sometime," she said. "Not now. I wouldn't dream of intruding on your day with Jeff. You're the one he wants to spend time with."

"You're right," Tracy said. "And I'm looking forward to it, even though I ought to be working on that article about my graduating class. It should have been done already."

"It'll wait. Besides, when we find out what's been going on aboard the good ship *Lucky Chance*, you might have a few more juicy tidbits to add to your story."

"That's what Jeff's been telling me."

"He's right," Amy said firmly. "So just enjoy being with him. Good guys like him are few and far between."

"He's a sweetheart, that's for sure."

Amy stood up. "Are you kids finished with your ice cream?"

"All done," Jana said, holding up both hands. "And I didn't make a mess."

"Good girl." Amy wiped a chocolate smudge from Jana's mouth. She glanced at Matt too, but only surreptitiously. He'd made it clear that he didn't like being fussed over in public. "How about we go to the grocery store and get everything we need to make dinner tomorrow?"

"I made a list when I was at school," Jana said. She fished a slightly grubby piece of paper out of her pocket and handed it to Amy.

Amy nodded as she read it over. "Good job, honey. It's always good to plan ahead. Are we ready to go?"

"Ready," Matt said, standing up. "Are you coming with us, Aunt Tracy?"

"Not today," Tracy said. "Uncle Jeff and I have a date. But I'll be there to help you tomorrow."

Jana giggled. "It's going to be fun, isn't it?"

"It sure is," Tracy said, and then she waved. "See you all later."

Jana giggled again, and Matt elbowed her not very subtly.

"Aunt Tracy should be here with Natalie and Colton in a few minutes," Amy said. "Are we ready?"

"I'm ready," Jana said, grinning. "I can't wait to cook."

"Where's your menu plan?" Amy asked her. They had gone over the plan again the night before, making sure the meal was at least somewhat balanced even if it was skewed heavily towards the kids' favorites.

"In my room," Jana said. "I took it to bed with me so I could look at it when I was falling asleep, and then this morning, I put it on my table so I would remember to bring it to the kitchen. I'll go get it."

By the time Tracy, Colton, and Natalie got to the house, everything was ready to go. The ingredients for each of the dishes were on the kitchen table along with mixing bowls, measuring cups and spoons, and baking pans.

"This ought to be easy," Tracy said approvingly. "I wish the kitchen elves would do this for me every time I make dinner."

She had assigned herself the role of cook's helper and kitchen tidier. And Amy was determined that, barring an actual problem, she and Tracy were there only in an advisory and instructional capacity. She started out by showing the children how to read a recipe, how to measure the ingredients, and how to set the oven and the stove at the right temperatures for the dishes they were making.

Matt seemed reasonably comfortable making simple dishes, so she let him take charge of the macaroni and cheese. Colton, on the other hand, seemed a little less sure about actually cooking, but he was right at home cutting up cheese and vegetables to put into the meat loaf.

"We don't usually have mushrooms and bell peppers in ours," he said, a curious look on his face very much like his dad's. "But we do have onions."

"Would you rather leave the mushrooms and peppers out?" Amy said. "We can, you know."

Colton considered that for a moment. "No, I guess it's okay. Dad likes them."

Matt gave him a startled look and then made his expression totally blank.

Amy waited for him to say something, but he went back to boiling macaroni.

"Is this right?" Natalie asked.

She looked very much the cook with her long, straight hair pulled back and one of Amy's aprons wrapped around her. She held up a tablespoon of black pepper, ready to dump it into the egg, milk, and cracker crumbs she and Jana had already mixed together.

"Whoa, whoa," Amy said. "Let's look at the recipe again. How much pepper does it say?"

The two girls looked at Grandma Pearl's cramped writing through the plastic page protector.

"It says one tisp," Natalie said, squinting at the spoon.

"T-s-p is the abbreviation for teaspoon," Amy said. "What kind of spoon do you have there?"

Natalie frowned, trying to read the spoon handle without dumping out its contents. "It says tabsp."

"That's tablespoon. It's abbreviated T-b-s-p. Tablespoon is the big one. Do you remember how many teaspoons are in a tablespoon?"

"Three," both girls said at once.

"That's right." Amy took the tablespoon from Natalie and returned the pepper to its jar. "So, if we're going to follow the recipe, what kind of spoon do you need?"

"A teaspoon," Natalie said.

Matt laughed at her. "Your dad won't like it if you mess it up." He stopped for a second and then ducked his head over the boiling pasta.

"You mean, if she cooks it for him at their house sometime," Tracy said, quickly passing him the milk.

Amy looked at her, but Tracy only smiled and appeared to be fascinated with the recipe for the pineapple upside-down cake they were about to make.

Before long they had everything mixed into the ground beef, and Amy let the girls very carefully put it into the oven. Matt put the macaroni and cheese into a baking dish and then put it on the stove, waiting until it was time to put it into the oven too. Seasoned green beans simmered away, and Colton had already measured out sliced almonds to put in them when they were ready. Then he and Matt put dinner rolls into a shallow pan, ready to brown them when the meat loaf was nearly done.

Finally, all four kids worked together to make the cake from another one of Grandma Pearl's old recipes. Amy and Tracy kept everything on track, but there was really very little they had to do.

"You're all doing great," Amy said, watching Natalie and Jana lay pineapple rings in the bottom of a cake pan while Matt mixed the cake batter and Colton added a cherry to the center of each pineapple ring.

"I'm impressed," Tracy said. "Everything is going to be delicious. Good job, everybody."

"So what do you think?" Amy asked. "Do you all like cooking?"

"It's fun," Colton said. "But it's a lot of work to do every day."

Amy chuckled. "This was kind of a special occasion. Most days it's a lot easier than this."

"But we had lots of people to help," Jana said. "So it wasn't very much to do."

"And now we know how to do it," Natalie said, "so we can when we want to."

"Just make sure you never turn on your oven or your stove unless your dad is there," Amy said. "Promise me you'll remember that, okay?"

Natalie nodded solemnly.

"Who's ready to set the table?" Tracy asked.

She handed down plates and silverware, not choosing Amy's special occasion dishes but not the everyday ones either. These were some their mother had liked, a soft blue with a woven pattern around the edges and delicate flowers here and there. Amy smiled to see them. Mom had given those to her when she was in college, and Amy had expected them to be for her first home once she was married. That hadn't worked out the way she had expected, but she loved the dishes anyway.

"We'll take care of it," Tracy said, reaching for the salt and pepper shakers. "You take everything out of the oven."

One of the things Amy had wanted to teach the children was to, as nearly as possible, have all the dishes come out at the same time so everything would be hot and ready to eat when everyone sat down. She was pleased to see that, apart from the rolls that needed about another minute or so, dinner was ready at seven on the dot. She wasn't so pleased when the doorbell rang at the same time.

"Ugh," she grumbled, setting the meat loaf on the stove. "I wasn't expecting anybody tonight."

"You go ahead and get it," Tracy said. "The kids and I will put everything on the table, and we can eat after you answer the door."

With a huff, Amy walked out of the kitchen, through the living room, into the wide entryway, and threw open the door. Then she froze.

Chapter Eighteen

*M*iles." Amy said, and then she managed a smile. "Uh, hi."

He looked very handsome standing there with his salt-and-pepper hair combed back and his square jaw freshly shaved. He wore a gray T-shirt under a navy-blue jacket and slim jeans that complemented his runner's frame.

He seemed puzzled for a moment and then glanced at his watch. "Did I get the time wrong? I thought it was supposed to be seven."

"Um, yes, we're eating at seven, but we haven't started yet. And Tracy was going to bring your kids home afterward. I know you had some things to do. I'm sorry you got out when you didn't have to."

"I, uh, yeah." He smiled uneasily. "I guess I got my signals crossed. I thought I was joining you."

She gaped at him. "You—" She scrambled to remember their exact conversation when they discussed the plans for tonight. What had she said that had gotten so mixed up? Suddenly, she smiled again. "I should have invited you, but I thought you were busy."

He chuckled. "And I decided I ought to be busy so you wouldn't think you'd have to invite me."

"Don't be silly," Amy said, laughing too as they walked toward the kitchen. "Of course you're welcome. And I hear you like meat loaf."

"Definitely. And yours smells wonderful."

"The kids made everything. Tracy and I just supervised. We made sure—" She stopped and looked around. The kitchen was empty. "I guess they're in the dining room already."

They walked around the corner to the dining room. Dinner was on the table, iced tea was poured into tall frosty glasses, and plates and silverware were laid out—but only for two.

"I don't understand," she said.

He nodded toward the note that was on one of the plates. "Maybe you'd better read that."

She picked it up and opened it, immediately recognizing Tracy's neat handwriting.

We're going for pizza. You and Miles enjoy your dinner. We'll be at my house when you're ready for us to come back.

It was signed with a little heart and nothing else.

Her face burning, Amy looked from the note to Miles's baffled face. "I—I'm sorry. I don't exactly know what's going on."

"I guess I'm confused too," he admitted. "Natalie told me yesterday that everybody wanted me to come at seven and join you for dinner. Man, I should have checked with you first. I didn't think anything of it. I'm sorry."

"I'm sorry too." Amy glanced at the note and then at the table full of food. "I hope you don't think I—I mean, I wouldn't want you to think I arranged all this just to get you over here alone."

"No, of course not," he said, and then one corner of his mouth turned up. "But I can't help wishing you had."

Did he mean what she hoped he meant?

"Maybe we'd better eat while it's hot."

The place settings were laid on one end of the table, one at the head and one close by, at the side. He pulled out a chair for her.

"Thanks," she said as she sat.

He took his place beside her. "Everything looks great."

They took a few minutes to fill their plates, making small talk as they did, mostly about how well the children had done making the meal. When they were ready to eat, Miles held out his hand.

"Do you want me to bless the meal?"

She slipped her hand into his and bowed her head, the warmth of his touch spreading all the way through her.

"Amen," she murmured when he was through, and then she watched as he took his first bite of the meat loaf.

"Wow," he said. "That's amazing. What all is in there?"

"That's how Grandma Pearl always made it," she told him, and then she listed the ingredients.

He took another eager bite. "Boy, have I been missing out all my life. I'm glad I came, even if you weren't expecting me."

Everything really did taste good, and Amy was glad the cooking lesson was such a success. Miles mentioned that, other than the meat loaf, he liked the mac and cheese best. Amy told him all about the kids' cooking adventure and how much everyone had enjoyed it. They talked a little about what she and Tracy had found out yesterday and about O'Shea being arrested for his involvement in Tracy's kidnapping. They didn't talk about being there together alone and whether or not there was any significance to the fact.

Finally, he ate the last of the green beans on his plate and sighed in satisfaction.

"You're a great teacher, and not just at math and reading."

"We had fun," she said. "And they did a really good job on everything."

"The cake too?" he said, eyeing it.

"They made that too. I think it turned out really nice."

"I bet it's delicious. Pineapple upside-down cake is my favorite, but I think I need a few minutes to digest dinner before I try it."

She nodded. "Not a problem. We can have coffee and cake a little later if you'd like. Unless you're in a hurry to get back home."

"Not at all."

"I know the invitation was a surprise to you," she said.

"And to you."

"Looks like we were both set up." An uncontrollable giggle bubbled out of her. "I knew they were up to something. But I never expected this."

"I didn't either," he said, and his expression was suddenly serious. "I've been thinking for a long time that we need to talk."

She took a drink of her iced tea to give herself a moment to think before she answered. He'd said he had wanted her to ask him over. Was it because he wanted more from their relationship? Or was it to make sure she understood that he still wanted to only be friends?

"Is there something in particular you wanted to talk about?" she asked, keeping her expression neutral.

"It's the kids. They seem to be spending more and more time together and, from what I can tell, really enjoying it."

"I think they are. You know Jana and Matt haven't had much in the way of family up until now, so I'm glad your kids have made them feel so welcome. That means a lot to me."

Miles nodded. "It means a lot to me too. Being a dad, especially being their only parent right now, I sometimes wonder if I'm teaching them the right things. I know Colton wasn't always very nice to Matt."

Amy smiled. "That was just at first. They're best friends now."

"Yeah, they are. And so are the girls."

"And that's because you've taught them a lot about kindness and acceptance and love. That means so much to Jana and Matt." She felt a tightness in her throat. "And to me."

"And that brings me to why I'm glad I came tonight…and why I'm glad it's just you and me." He took her hand again. "I wanted to talk about us."

"Us?"

She hoped he didn't notice the slightly higher pitch in her voice.

"I know it's been a very, very long time since we dated, and I guess I didn't handle our breakup all that well back then. I wasn't very mature at the time, and I didn't realize how much your freedom meant to you."

"Oh, Miles." She tightened her grip on his hand. "You were wonderful. I was the one who wasn't very mature. I thought I wanted to see the world, but when I decided to foster Matt and Jana, I realized all I really wanted was a home here in Canton and somebody I could love and trust to share it with me. But you'd moved on years ago." She picked up her napkin with her free hand and dabbed her eyes. "I'm sorry. I'm not trying to make you feel bad. It's not your fault, and I sure didn't expect you to stand around and wait for me to come to my senses."

"But have you?" he asked, his eyes as pleading as when he'd asked her not to leave all those years ago.

"Have I what?"

"Have you come to your senses?"

She looked away. "I have. Now, though, I'm wondering if it's too late."

"Amy—"

"I'd rather keep things the way they are and be your friend rather than scare you off by trying to make it something more."

"Amy." He put his free hand over their clasped ones. "I've been telling myself the same thing all these months."

She thought back on all the times she had thought it would be nice if they could rekindle their young romance, all the times he had put an arm around her and said how much he enjoyed spending time with her. She remembered too how she had told herself he was just being a friend. How she had reminded herself that he treated the kids the same way. Had he been waiting all this time for her to let him know she wanted more?

"I know I hurt you," she said softly. "I didn't know if it was too late for us to try again."

"Not if we don't want it to be."

"After all these years…"

"It's not how you start," he reminded her, "but how you finish."

Grow old along with me! The best is yet to be…

She hadn't thought of that poem in a very long time. Maybe it was too soon to think that way about them as a couple, but it could become a reality sometime down the road, couldn't it? Wasn't it true? Didn't the first part of life make people into who they became later on? Maybe the girl who had left Miles behind decades ago wouldn't have been happy with him if she had stayed. Maybe that girl had needed to have a wider look at the world before she, like Dorothy in *The Wizard of Oz*, could realize that her heart's desire had been right there in her own backyard all along.

She couldn't hold back a touch of a smile. "I guess we both needed a little nudge in the right direction."

He laughed, low and rumbly. "At least you figured out something was up. I didn't have the slightest idea that this was all a well-thought-out plan."

"Yep. And I have a good idea exactly who the mastermind was behind it all."

"Somebody I know?" he asked with a grin.

"I don't want to name names, but I have a feeling she's sitting at a table full of kids at the pizza parlor."

He nodded, his grin fading just slightly. "Speaking of kids, how do you think they'll feel about this? Have yours ever said anything to you? I mean about us? Together?"

She shook her head. "Not specifically. But I know they love you, and Matt has mentioned being a little jealous of Colton because he lives with his dad. Obviously, that's not possible for Matt. Even if he wasn't in prison, Matt's dad has no interest in having a relationship with him."

"I'm sorry," Miles said. "That's hard on a kid."

"He and Jana have had a hard time all their lives, and since I adopted them, I've wanted them to have as much security and stability as I can give them. I don't want them to think that if I do start dating someone, they'd suddenly be pushed to the side. They don't talk about it much, but I get the impression that whenever their mother had a boyfriend, they were pretty much on their own."

"It's a balance, isn't it," he said. "Any couple has to make sure their kids have plenty of attention while not neglecting their own relationship. Our kids have been the center of parental attention for a while. I'm sure there'll be some adjustment when they have to share the spotlight with someone else." He squeezed her hand a little more tightly. "But I think we can work it so nobody feels left out."

She nodded, her eyes fixed on his earnest ones. He was such a kind man. A good and thoughtful man. He was already a good father, and a good father was something her kids needed. Just like his kids needed a good mother.

"If I hadn't been so oblivious," he said with a chuckle, "this wouldn't have come as such a surprise to me. Looking back, I remember a few little things they've said. Natalie's mentioned a couple of times how nice you are and about how much fun it would be if you went clothes shopping with her like you do with Jana."

"We can do that. I don't know why I haven't thought of it before. I bet the girls would have a blast picking things out together." Amy paused. "I don't suppose Colton has said anything."

"Not in so many words, but he's always happy when he and Natalie get to come over here to play with your two. He's got an image to protect, so he doesn't say much about wanting a mom in the house, but there are times I can tell he'd like to have one. Even if he doesn't want to admit it, he's still a little boy in some ways."

Amy smiled. That was so like Matt, wanting to be seen as tough but still needing a mother's love and reassurance.

"All our kids come from broken families in one way or another," she said. "Maybe, between us, we can give them a little more of what they need."

"And a little of what we need. We're not just parents."

"True."

"So..." He looked at her for a long moment and then he lifted her hand. "Are you ready for take two?"

She reached over with her free hand and caressed his cheek. "I'll try not to blow it this time."

He leaned closer, kissed her, and then wrapped her in his arms.

"I've been wanting to do that for a long time," he murmured against her hair.

"I'm glad you finally did."

"Next time you talk to Tracy," he said, amusement in his tone, "tell her I said thank you."

"I'll tell her, although she might be a little hard to live with for the next few days."

They took the coffee and pieces of cake into the living room where they could be more relaxed while they talked. It seemed natural to have him there with her, their comfortable relationship feeling deeper now that they had finally admitted what for a long while had been in their hearts. Though she knew he was right, she felt a twinge of sadness when he finally said it was time he got Colton and Natalie home again.

He kissed her temple. "We've all got church in the morning. Matt and Jana need their sleep too."

"You're right. Do you want to have lunch with us afterward? We have a lot of leftovers, and the kids never even got to taste any of their culinary creations."

"I thought you usually have lunch at Tracy's on Sundays."

"Usually, but tomorrow Jeff's taking her to the county fair in Wayland to spend the afternoon."

"Okay, sure," Miles said. "Everything was really good, and I wouldn't mind seconds at all."

"Good. I'll call Tracy."

Tracy picked up her call immediately. "I wondered when I was going to hear from you."

"Uh-huh," Amy said. "I'm sure you want to know how your little scheme worked out."

Tracy laughed. "It wasn't only me, you know. The kids had the idea about making dinner for you and Miles. I just agreed to help them with the details. But as much as I want to hear how it went, I have some news to tell you. Are you sitting down?"

"Yeah. Miles and I are sitting on the couch. Can I put you on speaker?"

"Sure. I have a favor to ask both of you anyway."

Amy tapped the speaker icon and then set the phone on the coffee table. "Can you hear me okay?"

"Perfect," Tracy said. "Miles, do you have anything you need to do tomorrow after church? Or can you do something for me?"

"I'll be happy to help if I can," Miles said. "What is it?"

"I talked to Eve a little while ago," Tracy said. "I went ahead and asked her if she knew where Fran was on Thursday afternoon when the yearbook was stolen. Eve didn't know. She said they'd had a big fight when Eve caught her snooping around her room. She asked Danny, and he said Fran was in a meeting with him about the wardrobe budget all afternoon on Thursday, so it looks like she couldn't have been our yearbook thief."

"That takes her off the list," Amy said. "I thought for sure she was up to something."

"And," Tracy said, "Lyle has bought a new screen for the play."

"Really?" Amy said. "I thought he was a cheapskate and that's why Eve borrowed ours."

"True," Tracy said, "but it seems Rudy's agreed to invest in the play, and he wants to make a few upgrades to the production. He likes Grandma Pearl's screen, but he didn't think the show should be responsible for it, so he found something similar."

"Well, good," Amy said. "To be honest, I'd rather have the screen back at your house and not have to think about the *Lucky Chance* any more than we have to at this point."

"But that's not the biggest part of what I found out," Tracy said, sounding almost breathless. "It looks like getting investment money from Rudy isn't what Lyle is going to have on his mind right now. The police just arrested him."

hat?" Amy gasped, staring at her phone as if she could see her sister's face through it. "It was Lyle all along?"

Miles's eyes widened.

"Dale called me a few minutes after I talked to Eve," Tracy said. "That man he arrested at the café yesterday, O'Shea, confessed that Lyle hired him and Montez to do the kidnapping while Lyle had an alibi in Vegas."

"But why?" Amy asked. "Why would he want to kidnap you?"

"They don't know that yet. O'Shea doesn't know. He was just paid to do a job, and Lyle is still saying he had nothing to do with the kidnapping."

"Wow." Amy sighed. "I really don't get that. You never met him before the other day, did you?"

"Never," Tracy said. "Never even heard of him till we went to see Eve last Saturday. I doubt he'd ever heard of me either, and I can't think of anything I've written or am planning to write for the paper that would upset him. It's weird."

"The police will get to the bottom of it," Miles said. "But you've got to feel better about them at least finding out who was behind the kidnapping."

"I do," Tracy agreed. "And Jeff's really relieved to hear it too. Dale made it sound like Lyle is a good possibility. They just have to figure out what his motive was. It seems senseless at this point."

"So what can I do to help?" Miles asked her.

"Well," Tracy said, "since they have another screen to use for the play, I'd like to get ours back. Things are kind of up in the air about the show now that it looks like Lyle may be in custody for some time. Eve tells me Rudy is planning to step in and keep things going for now, but the production doesn't seem very stable at the moment. I'd feel better if we got the screen back right away."

"And you want us to pick it up," Amy said, looking to see Miles's reaction.

"Could you?" Tracy asked. "To be honest, I'd really like to be completely done with the *Lucky Chance* entirely. I'm committed to writing my article, but after that, I'll be glad to never think about it or anybody on it ever again."

"I understand," Miles said. "And, sure, Amy and I will be happy to get it back. Tomorrow?"

"If you could," Tracy said. "Jeff and I are going to be gone all day. Amy and I could get it on Monday, but we couldn't do it until she was out of school, and I'd rather not wait that long."

"Tomorrow should be fine," he told her. "I just have to get somebody to look after my kids."

"Mine too," Amy said. "I hate to bother Robin again, but I can call Olivia and see if she's free. She watches Matt and Jana all the time. I'm sure she won't mind adding Natalie and Colton and making a little extra money."

"Thank you," Tracy said. "I feel a little silly asking you, especially you, Miles, but it really would make me feel better. I don't know…" She sighed. "I feel like I need closure on the whole experience."

Amy could see how Tracy would need that. "We'll take care of it," she promised.

"I know it's a pain, but do you think you could bring the screen back to my place? You have a key."

"Not a problem at all. You and Jeff go and have a good time. Buy me something good for Christmas, okay?"

Tracy laughed. "You never know."

"Bring the kids when you're ready," Amy said. "You can help me put the leftovers away."

"Be there in the few minutes," Tracy said, and she ended the call.

"Are you sure you don't mind helping me with the screen?" Amy asked Miles.

"I'm sure. If the kids and I are having lunch over here, then your sitter can come and watch the kids while we get the screen."

"Let me call Olivia and see if she's available."

Olivia was in fact available for the next afternoon and happy to earn a little money, even though Amy and Miles weren't likely to be gone very long.

"We're set," Amy said after she ended the call.

"Good," Miles said. "And I was thinking that we can even put the screen up in the attic for Tracy if you want. That'll save her and Jeff the trouble."

"Good idea." She leaned over and kissed his cheek. "I think I'm going to like having you around."

"Aw, shucks, ma'am," he said, pulling her into his arms for a proper kiss.

Tracy and the kids showed up about five minutes later, all of them grinning and smug about how they had arranged Miles and Amy's "date."

"We don't know that it ended up being a date," Tracy said to the kids. "Though they still look like they like each other."

"We get along just fine, thank you," Miles said, putting his arm around Amy. "And if any of you object to us seeing more of each other, you'd better speak up now."

"I'm not speaking up, Dr. Miles," Jana said, her eyes shining.

He tapped her nose. "I knew I could count on you."

Natalie slipped over to Amy's side and put one arm around her waist.

"What about all the food we made?" Matt asked, hands on his hips.

"You can't be hungry," Tracy said. "Not after all the pizza you just ate."

"No," Matt said. "But there has to be some left over for tomorrow or something."

"We didn't even get to taste it," Colton said. "Did you save some for us, Miss Amy?"

"We sure did," Amy said. "And everybody's coming back here after church to eat it. How's that?"

"Do you want us to help you put everything away before we go?" Miles asked her.

"Tracy will help me," Amy said. "She was behind all this in the first place. You'd better take Natalie and Colton home so they can get ready for bed."

"Good night," Miles said, giving her a quick peck on the cheek. Colton rolled his eyes.

Miles gave him a nudge toward the door and then took his daughter's hand. "Come on. We'll see everybody tomorrow."

Once they were gone, Tracy and the kids cleared the dining room table. Amy picked up the cake plates and coffee cups and carried them into the kitchen.

"You two go ahead and start getting ready for bed," Amy said to Matt and Jana. "Church tomorrow."

"Is Dr. Miles going to be our new dad?" Jana asked as she handed Tracy the nearly empty tea glasses.

"Whoa," Amy said, smiling in spite of herself. "It's way too early to wonder about that. Right now, he and I are going to go on some dates and spend time together and see how things go. And we can't just think of ourselves, you know. We have you and Matt and Natalie and Colton to consider too. It might take a while for us to be sure we're making the right decision."

"But what do you think?" Jana insisted.

"Dr. Miles and I haven't even talked about that yet," Amy told her. "It's a big decision for all of us. What do *you* think?"

"We talked about it," Jana said matter-of-factly. "We like it. Well, mostly we like it. Colton isn't sure yet."

Amy glanced at Tracy, who gave her a puzzled shrug in return.

"Colton just has to think about it," Matt said. "He remembers his mom more than Natalie does, and I think he's still kinda sad about her. But he really likes you, Mom. He just isn't sure how it would be if we all lived together." He winced slightly. "I guess I'm not either."

Amy put her arm around him. "That's why we're not making any big decisions right this minute, okay? Dr. Miles and I are going to see how things work out. But if either of you don't like the idea at this point, we need to talk about that and find out why. I want you both to be honest with me. I promise I won't be mad."

"It's not that we don't like it," Matt said. "It's just another big change. Again."

Amy hugged him. "I know it hasn't been easy for you and Jana, but I promise I'll never do anything that I think won't be good for both of you, okay?"

He gave her a hug, and then he squirmed away. "Come on, Jana. We have to get to bed."

"I'll be up to tell you good night in a few minutes," Amy told them.

"And I'll see you both later." Tracy gave them each a hug. "I'm glad our little plan worked."

"Me too." Jana kissed her on the cheek. "Good night."

"Good night, Aunt Tracy," Matt said, and they both headed upstairs.

Tracy rinsed the dishes and put them in the dishwasher while Amy put plastic wrap over the leftovers. Neither of them said anything, and that gave Amy a minute to think. She hadn't expected to have to make any kind of decision about Miles tonight, but that didn't mean she hadn't considered the effect their dating and potential marriage might have on her kids and his.

Both of the girls were younger, so maybe it was easier for them to accept a new parent. Were the boys ready? She knew Matt liked Miles, but was he ready to have Miles be his father? And what about

Colton? He had seemed as happy as the other children when she and Miles had told them they were going to start dating, but how did he feel about something more permanent?

Tracy turned off the faucet, and the kitchen was quiet. "You're worried about Colton, aren't you?"

"Do you think he'd rather Miles and I didn't see each other?"

"I think he's like anybody else. Change is scary, especially such a big change. But I don't think that means he's against the idea. Maybe it didn't seem real to him until you and Miles actually said you were going to start dating."

Amy started putting the covered dishes into the refrigerator. "I hope he'll talk to Miles about it if it really bothers him."

"He already has."

Amy stopped what she was doing, the refrigerator door still open. "He has?"

Tracy smiled. "I don't think you actually understand how all this happened. Let's finish up here and have some tea."

"Okay."

Tracy fixed the tea while Amy finished putting the food away. Then they both sat at the kitchen table.

"None of this was my idea," Tracy began. "The kids talked about it between themselves first. I think it was Natalie who realized her dad liked you but didn't want to say anything yet. She asked Jana if you liked him, and Jana said she thought you did, but *you* didn't want to say anything either. So they talked to the boys a couple of weeks ago when they were all over at Miles's house. They decided if they got you two to have dinner together, you might both decide you liked it."

Amy giggled. "A real parent trap."

"Yup. Jana told me about what they wanted to do, and I said I'd help. I hope you're happy about it."

Amy sighed, knowing there had to be a goofy grin on her face. "Really happy. I've always loved Miles. When I walked away from him, I was too young to realize guys like him didn't come along every day."

"Don't beat yourself up over it. Just be thankful for another chance."

"I definitely am, but things sure are more complicated now than they were when we were fresh out of school."

Tracy chuckled. "It worked out all right for the Brady Bunch."

Amy gave her a wry look. "There's some profound and practical wisdom."

"It's way too early to be thinking so hard about all this. Just enjoy what it is right now, okay?"

Amy nodded. "You're right, and I am. So when are you and Jeff leaving tomorrow?"

"Straight after church. We decided we'd eat lunch somewhere in Wayland and then go to the fair. I'm really looking forward to it. Thanks for taking care of the screen for me."

"No problem. It'll give me and Miles a little more time alone together, and I know he likes to help when he can. What's important is that you and Jeff have a good time and don't worry about the screen or about the case anymore. The police will figure out what they need to know. And at the least we know the bad guys are locked up, Lyle and his two thugs."

"True," Tracy said. "I'm going to enjoy my afternoon with my husband and let you and Miles take care of tying up the last loose end."

They finished tidying up the kitchen and said good night. Afterward, Amy went upstairs to check on the kids. Jana was already cuddled up with her dolls, fast asleep. Matt was in bed but still had his light on.

"How was the pizza tonight?" Amy asked.

One corner of Matt's mouth turned up. "It was good. We had a lot of fun fixing things up for you and Dr. Miles."

"You were all very sweet to do it."

He shrugged. "We figured neither of you would ever say anything if we didn't."

She kissed his cheek, told him good night, and turned off the light, knowing she would never get a stronger endorsement from him than that.

After church the next day, all four kids enjoyed finally getting to eat the meal they had made the night before, and Miles didn't seem to mind having leftovers. While they were having dessert, Olivia showed up to watch the kids, so Amy gave her a piece of pineapple upside-down cake and told her she and Miles would be back as soon as they could.

As soon as they got into Miles's car, he leaned over and gave Amy a kiss.

"I've been wanting to do that since last night."

She smiled at him. "I've been wanting you to do that for a long time before then."

He laughed. "We'll have to catch up on all we've missed out on since high school. For now, though, we'd better get that screen back to Tracy's house. Then we can figure out what to do with four kids who just got a sugar overload."

When they pulled up to the *Lucky Chance*, Amy was surprised to see a police car parked out front.

"I wonder what's going on."

"I guess we'll find out," Miles said. "Come on."

Nobody questioned them as they went aboard. There were no deckhands in sight. Nobody was around at all.

"It feels a little creepy," Amy said.

Miles nodded, and they stepped into the lobby.

"Hello?" he called. "Anybody here?"

The door leading into the theater opened, and Eve peered out.

"Oh, Amy," she said, coming out to them. "Good. I'm glad it's you. Tracy told me you'd be coming to pick up the screen. This must be Dr. Miles. Hello, I'm Eve Sendry."

Miles shook her hand. "Miles Anderson."

"What's going on with the police?" Amy asked her. "Anything wrong?"

"What isn't wrong?" Eve put a hand over her heart. "Fran still isn't speaking to me, though I suppose I should see that as a bonus, and I'm sure Tracy told you about Lyle. It's shocking. That police-man, Officer Leewright, is in Lyle's office now, warrant and all, looking for evidence about the kidnapping."

"Where is everybody?" Amy asked. "There are usually a couple of deckhands around if nobody else."

"The officer has everybody gathered backstage while the office is being searched," Eve explained. "He didn't want anybody sneaking away. Danny's babysitting, but he let me come see who was at the door."

Rudy came in from the deck, as unflappable as usual. "It doesn't look quite as terrible as you described it to me," he said to Eve. "Amy. How are you?"

"All right," Amy said. "This is Miles Anderson. Miles, this is Rudy Daheim. He's the one who was interested in financing and expanding Lyle's operation."

The two men shook hands.

"Does this change your investment plans?" Miles asked.

Rudy gave him pleasantly baffled smile. "Of course not. There is a great deal the police have yet to uncover about this case. I don't want to make any rash decisions before we know all the facts. Lyle still denies being involved in the kidnapping or anything else criminal, and I have no reason to doubt him. When I back someone, it's because I believe in him." He put his arm around Eve. "Or her. No use spoiling a good business opportunity over nothing."

"True," Amy said. "Well, we'd better get the screen and get going. Miles's kids and mine are waiting for us."

"Let me help," Rudy said, and they all went up on stage.

The new screen, intricately carved mahogany, was a vast improvement over the cheap original, but it still couldn't hold a candle to Grandma Pearl's. Hers was leaning against the back wall, already strapped up so it wouldn't flap open while it was being moved. Before the two men could lift it, Dale came into the theater.

He looked at Eve disapprovingly. "I thought you were supposed to stay put."

"Somebody had to come see who came aboard," she said. "Nobody's removing any evidence, and I already told you somebody was coming to pick up this screen."

Dale nodded. "Amy. Miles."

"Good to see you, Dale," Miles said, shaking his hand.

"We'd like to know more about what you've found out about Lyle," Amy said to Dale. "Tracy said he denies having anything to do with the kidnapping."

"He does," Dale said, "but things aren't looking good for him. One thing we found in his office that'll interest you is your sister's missing yearbook."

Chapter Twenty

"What?" Rudy gasped.

Amy looked at him, equally baffled, and he cleared his throat.

"What would he be doing with that?" Rudy asked. "How could he have gotten it? And why would he want it?"

"Obviously, he could have gotten it when Tracy and Amy were talking to you and Eve the day it was stolen," Dale said. "Who knows why he'd want it?"

"It just seems very strange," Rudy said. "If he wanted a yearbook like that, he could have taken Eve's anytime."

"I hadn't thought of that," Eve said, "but it's true. He knew it was there. I showed him and Fran some of the pictures from our plays that ended up in the book."

"Is it still there?" Dale asked her.

"Yes, of course," Eve said. "At least it was last night. I showed Rudy some of my pictures too. And they arrested Lyle before that."

Amy frowned. Why would Lyle have gone to the trouble of breaking into Tracy's house to get her yearbook when he could so easily have taken Eve's?

"Tracy's away from home today," she told Dale. "Do you think I could have the yearbook to give back to her?"

"Sorry," Dale said. "That has to stay in evidence."

"I understand, but she's going to be so disappointed. She needs that book for her article."

"Can't she borrow Eve's?" Miles suggested.

Amy shook her head. "It wouldn't be the same. She specifically wanted to use some of the autographs in her own as kind of headers for each person's story."

"Wish I could help you," Dale said. "Though I could probably get you copies of the pages she wants. Would that help?"

"I'm sure it would," Amy said. "Can I get them right away?"

"I have a copier, if you want to use it," Eve offered.

"That'll work," Dale said. "You tell me what you need, and I'll get you copies."

"Tracy should be home early this evening," Amy said after she had given him a list of names. "She'll be happy to get them."

"I'll get somebody to take care of it right away."

Rudy watched as Dale walked backstage again. "Must be nice to have a friend on the force. He probably wouldn't have done that for anybody else."

"We've been friends a long time," Amy said. "He's a great guy."

"And Tracy can still write her wonderfully flattering article," Rudy said, breaking into a sunny smile. "Crisis averted. Now, what about the reason for your visit?"

He and Miles picked up the screen, prepared to carry it to the car, and then put it down again when Eve's son shoved his way past them to get to her.

"Excuse us," Miles said half under his breath.

"Mom, I need to talk to you." Flynn clutched an envelope in one hand, and his cheeks were a patchy red. "Right now."

"Oh, darling, I know." Eve came over and kissed his forehead. "It's your birthday, and here I am tied up with all the craziness going on here. You'll never believe it, but Lyle was arrested just a little while ago. Arrested! And I told Rudy—"

"This is serious, and I need to talk to you in private."

"Of course, of course, darling. I know, it's so disappointing, but I'll make it up to you, I promise."

"Mother—"

"I'm sorry, Flynn," Eve said, her words coming more and more rapidly, "but I can't leave right now. The police are searching the boat, and everyone is supposed to stay here. We'll have our party, but it may have to be tomorrow or the next day. That'll be all right, won't it?"

"No, it won't."

"Darling—"

"You've put me off and put me off, and we're having this out right now." Flynn snatched some folded pages out of the envelope, snapped them open, and held them up. "I want to know what this is all about. These were in my mailbox this afternoon."

"Maybe we should go," Miles murmured to Amy.

"No," Eve said, her shoulders sagging. "Stay. You're going to hear about it anyway."

Amy went to her, sure she already knew what had happened. "What's wrong?"

"Flynn's trust," Eve said, her lower lip trembling. "It's all gone."

She gave Amy the papers, but Amy only glanced at them before handing them back. The account wasn't completely empty, but there was no way Flynn and his wife-to-be were going to buy a house and start a business with what was left.

"How could you?" Flynn asked.

"Flynn, baby..." Eve reached toward him. "I didn't mean for it to get this bad. Honestly. I was only borrowing. I mean, that's how it started. I was going to pay it all back. If you had only given me a little more time, I would have. I promise."

"Out of what?" Flynn demanded, snatching the papers from her. "I know how you are. You've never saved or invested a dime of what you made, and you still live like you're an A-lister in Hollywood. How in the world did you ever imagine you could pay this back?"

Eve looked at him hopelessly, her eyes filled with tears.

"I was going to help her," Rudy said, coming to her side. "I've been arranging funds for investing in this project, and I told her I could make her a loan to tide her over."

Eve clutched his arm, her tears spilling, and then she reached toward her son. "I'm so sorry, baby. Please forgive me. Please."

Flynn clenched his jaw, and his chin quivered. "Mom, how could you?" Before she could say anything, he held up one hand to stop her. "It doesn't matter, okay? It's done. I'll deal with it."

Before she could say anything else, he was gone.

Eve turned and buried her face against Rudy's shoulder. "Oh, Flynn."

"We'll make it right," Rudy said gently. "Don't let it worry you. I told you I'd stand by you, didn't I?"

She nodded, blotted her face with a tissue from her pocket, and then put on a bright smile. "You did. And he'll forgive me. He always does." She glanced toward the door Flynn had just gone through. "In time."

Amy tried to pity her but couldn't help thinking of all the hopes and dreams her son had built up around the trust that had been left to him. It was a cruel blow for him to have to take, especially on his birthday.

"Oh, why did he have to see those statements now?" Eve said, pacing. "Just another day or two, and it wouldn't have mattered. I would've gotten the money from Rudy and paid the trust fund back."

"Where did you keep them?" Amy asked, thinking there could have been only one person who would have sent those pages to Flynn.

"In my cabin, of course," Eve said, and then her eyes narrowed. "That little sneak."

"What?" Rudy asked. "Who?"

"Fran, of course." Eve started pacing again. "She was smirking at me this morning when I saw her in the corridor. I caught her sneaking around my room earlier in the week, but I didn't see anything out of place. I even looked to see if those statements were where I left them, but she must have made copies. She knew Flynn would show up here when he got them. I'll get her for that."

"Don't do anything stupid," Amy said. "Like Flynn said, it's done now. Let everybody cool down before you do anything, okay?"

Eve pursed her lips, but didn't agree to anything.

"We'd better put the screen in the car and get home," Miles told Amy. "The kids are waiting for us."

"You're right," Amy said. "Let me get those copies, and we can go."

"I'll get them for you," Rudy volunteered, but before he could take more than a couple of steps, Dale came from backstage, copies in hand.

"Here you go," he said, handing the pages to Amy. "These ought to hold Tracy over until we can return her yearbook to her."

"We really ought to go, Amy," Miles said, glancing at his watch. "This was supposed to be a quick trip."

"It did get a little complicated," Amy said. "We'd better get the screen loaded."

"Let me help," Rudy said. "I'm sure Miles and I can take care of it."

"Thanks," Amy said. "That would be great."

"Thanks for being so kind, Amy," Eve said.

"I hope you and Flynn work things out."

She didn't dare bring up Fran at this point.

Eve gave her a tentative smile. "Well, if I don't see you before we leave Canton, best of luck."

Miles and Rudy picked up the screen, and Amy followed them out to the car. It took only a minute or two for the men to load the screen and secure it, but before Miles could even thank Rudy for his help, his phone rang.

"Gotta take this," Miles told Rudy once he looked at his phone. "It's the clinic. Hello?"

While Miles talked, Rudy turned to Amy. "He must be a busy man."

"He is," Amy said, watching the concern on Miles's face. "He's a good doctor."

"I'm sure," Rudy said, and then he nodded toward the handful of papers she carried. "I'm really looking forward to reading Tracy's article too. She wrote a great story about what happened to her last week. She's a good writer."

"She definitely is," Amy said, keeping half of her attention on Miles's expressions. Something serious was going on. "She's a good investigative reporter too. It might take her a while to put the pieces together, but she always does. Maybe these pages will nudge her in the right direction."

"I'm sure they will," Rudy said.

"I'm sorry, Amy," Miles said after he ended his call. "I've got a situation I have to take care of. I have to make a house call. This little girl gets hysterical at the hospital, and her mom doesn't know if she really needs to go to the ER or if there's something I can do for her at home. They're both very upset, and I'm hoping I can get them calmed down."

"Of course you need to go," Amy said. "What about the screen?"

"We can put it in my car," Rudy said. "I can drive you wherever it is you're taking it."

"I don't have time for that," Miles said. "Now that the screen is in my car, it'll be just as easy to drop Amy off at home. It's on the way from here, and we can take the screen to Tracy's later." He turned to Amy. "Do you mind if the kids stay with you a little longer?"

"Not a problem," Amy said.

"I'll let you go then," Rudy said. "Are you sure that's secure?"

He moved toward the car just as Miles turned to look at the screen, and the two of them bumped into each other.

"That was clumsy of me," Rudy said. "I'm so sorry."

Miles shook his head and then glanced at his watch. "I'm afraid I wasn't paying attention. Amy, we'd better get going."

Rudy shook his hand. "Good luck to both of you. Be careful on the road."

Miles and Amy got into the car. Rudy waved as they drove away. Before long, they were at Amy's.

"I can't stay," he told his disappointed kids. "Got an emergency, but I'll be back as quick as I can."

He hugged Colton and Natalie, and then Amy walked with him to his car.

"We'll be here when you get through," she said. "Call me."

"I will." He patted his pocket, and then he frowned. "Aw, man, where's my phone? I had it at the boat."

"It must be in the car." Amy opened the driver-side door to look.

Miles put his hand over hers. "I don't have time to backtrack and look for it, but I will when I get a chance." He gave her a quick kiss. "See you soon."

"Okay," she said, wishing he didn't have to go. "We'll be here."

She watched him until his car was out of sight, and then she went back into the house. Olivia was coming out of the kitchen with a tray of cookies and some juice boxes.

"Hey," Amy said, helping herself to a cookie. "Where's that going?"

"I hope it's okay with you," Olivia said. "We pulled out the Lego set Matt got last year, and we're putting it together."

"That huge thing?" Amy chuckled. "Where'd you put it?"

"We were going to do it at the kitchen table, but we decided it would be in the way next time you ate, so we moved it to the floor in the guest room."

"That'll work."

Jana ran out of the guest room and hugged Amy's waist. "Mom! Come see!"

She grabbed Amy's hand and pulled her into the room. There were Legos all over the carpet and around the beginnings of a very impressive castle.

"Nice," Amy said. "You've all been busy. Olivia, you can go ahead and go, if you'd like. How much do I owe you?"

Olivia gave her a sheepish grin. "Actually, is it okay if I stay just a little while longer? We're about to set up the drawbridge, and I want to make sure it works."

Amy chuckled. "Sure. Stay as long as you want."

"Thanks," Olivia said. She got down on the floor next to Matt. "Do you have the pieces ready?"

Amy looked at the five of them, busily working away, and thought how nice it was to have a babysitter who not only took care of the kids but played with them too.

She went into the kitchen and fixed herself a cup of coffee, and then she sat down to go over her lesson plan for the next day. The weekend was nearly over already. She hoped Miles and his kids would stay awhile after he got back. Maybe they could all watch a movie or play a game before they had to go home.

About twenty minutes later, her phone dinged, and she smiled to see she had a text from Miles.

HEY!

HEY! she typed back. GLAD YOU FOUND YOUR PHONE! EVERY-THING OK WITH YOUR PATIENT?

NOTHING SERIOUS. HAD AN IDEA ABOUT TRACY'S KIDNAPPING. CAN YOU MEET ME AT ROBERT'S BOATHOUSE?

She frowned. The boathouse?

WHAT'S GOING ON? WHAT'S AT THE BOATHOUSE?

I'LL EXPLAIN THERE. NEED YOU TO HURRY. THINK I SOLVED THE CASE. BRING THE COPIES.

WHY? CALL ME.

He answered swiftly. RUNNING OUT OF CHARGE. MEET ME HERE. BRING COPIES. WILL EXPLAIN.

Her frown deepening, she called his number and immediately got his voice mail. His phone must have totally run down. Still, if he had learned something that solved the case, she definitely wanted to know about it. When he went back to the *Lucky Chance* to look for his phone, he must have come across something that was tied to Tracy being taken to Robert's boathouse. Something that finally made sense out of everything.

She put her phone down and returned to the guest room.

"I'm sorry, Olivia. Things have changed again. Can you stay with the kids a little while longer?"

"Sure," Olivia said. "Is everything okay?"

All four kids looked at Amy anxiously.

"Everything's fine," she assured them. "I have to go meet Dr. Miles, but we should be back really soon. You be good for Olivia, okay?"

She got a chorus of okays from the group and then hurried out to the car, the photocopies of Tracy's yearbook in hand. What could Miles have figured out?

As she drove, she glanced over at the copies on the passenger seat. How could those autographs from over thirty-five years ago have anything to do with what had happened to Tracy? But they almost had to. They were literally the only thing that made Tracy's yearbook different from Eve's.

She considered each one as she sat at a stoplight. Dave Winston, the awkward boy who'd gone on to become a giant in the tech industry, had written a simple *Best*.

Photos of the twins Tony and Mike Hernandez had, of course, been printed side by side. Mike had signed his *Double*, and Tony had signed his *Trouble*.

Bryan Ulmer, the boy who'd been in and out of trouble and who'd eventually been lost in the tragedy of 9/11, had written *Voted most likely to end up rich or in jail. HA!*

Amy had already seen what Tracy's early theater crush, Chris Marks, had written by his admittedly handsome photo. *Off Broadway, but not for long!* And then there was Eve's as Kitty McAllen. *Hollywood, here I come!*

What did these signatures have to do with where those people were today? Eve had ended up in Hollywood, at least briefly. Chris had indeed made it on Broadway. There was nothing in Dave's bland comment or in the twins' or even in poor Bryan's that could possibly be damaging to anyone today. What had Miles found that made them relevant?

The light changed, and Amy started down the road again, thinking about the handwriting each of them had used. It all seemed fairly typical for teens at the time. Eve's was round and splashy, Chris's large and almost art deco looking, Bryan's spiky and off-kilter, almost like the credits in an old scary movie. The twins probably had the best penmanship, their letters clear and well formed, while Dave's writing was small and cramped and nearly illegible.

Eve was the only person who seemed connected to Tracy's article, her yearbook, and the boat Tracy was kidnapped from, but she still seemed to have no motive for the kidnapping, especially if Tracy truly had been the intended victim. Sure, Eve had gotten herself into trouble with her son's trust, but kidnapping Tracy certainly wouldn't have made her troubles any less troubling. And if Tracy had been taken by mistake, what did the yearbook have to do with it?

She pulled up in front of the boathouse, glad it was still daylight. When she'd been here the last time, several people, including a police officer, were with her, and she hadn't particularly noticed how isolated it was. She noticed it now.

She didn't like the feeling she was getting. If Miles was here, where was his car? Had something happened to him? Maybe she'd better check inside. If he was in there and had run into trouble, he might need help.

She turned off the engine and went to the door. The latch had been replaced since Tracy was brought here, but it wasn't fastened. There was no padlock. She swung the door open.

"Miles?"

Someone was inside, but she couldn't see him in the dimness. She was sure it wasn't Miles.

"Who's there?" she asked.

The man stepped into the light that came in through the doorway.

"Hello, Amy."

Chapter Twenty-One

*A*my took a step back from the boathouse. "Rudy. What are you doing here?"

Rudy came through the door and gave her his usual placid smile. She noticed he had his right hand in his jacket pocket. "Waiting for you. Won't you come in?"

"Where's Miles? I was supposed to meet him here."

"I understand he's dealing with an emergency. Did you bring the copies of the yearbook pages?"

She took another step back, wondering if she could make it to the car.

"You picked Miles's pocket and stole his phone when we were at the *Lucky Chance*. He never texted me at all."

"That's true." Rudy made a subtle gesture with the hand that was in his pocket. "This doesn't have to become difficult. Go on in."

She held her ground.

"Please," he said mildly. "You have a family that loves you. Children who need you. And the gallant Dr. Anderson seems to like having you around. You wouldn't want to disappoint any of them."

She lifted her chin. "What do you want?"

"I want you to give me the copies and go into the boathouse. Don't make it any more difficult than it needs to be. I have no interest in hurting you. Please don't force me into it."

He gestured again with the hand in his pocket. What did he have in there? A gun? A knife? Nothing? She wasn't about to risk her life to find out, especially if all he wanted was the copies.

She handed them over. "The police have the originals of these, you know."

"I realize that." He gestured toward the door again. "But that won't matter in a few hours."

She had to keep calm. The copies didn't matter at this point. She was in no position to keep him from getting away, but maybe she could find out what this was about.

She went inside, and Rudy pulled the string to turn on the one bare light bulb hanging from the ceiling. A boat, presumably Robert West's, was moored there. The place looked pretty much like it had right after Tracy's kidnapping, except now there was a folding chair in one corner. Had he been sitting there waiting for her?

"You have the copies," she said. "Why don't you just go now?"

"No, that would be a little too quick to suit my purposes. It's all about timing at this point, so I'm going to have to ask you to be patient for a little while. Again, I'm not going to hurt you unless you give me problems, so please don't."

"What's this all about?"

She glanced around the boathouse, trying to find some way to get away from him, and noticed something underneath the chair. It was a wide roll of black electrical tape. Her stomach clenched.

"You're the one who had Tracy kidnapped, aren't you?" She licked her lips, praying hard for some way out. "Why? And why did you let her go?"

Rudy smiled. "No, as a matter of fact, I had nothing to do with that, but it did give me a good idea of what to do with you."

"But why? Why do you want those copies? What good are they to you? You didn't go to that school."

He looked amused. "I'm sure the police will figure it out in time. After I'm gone. Your sister was on her way to figuring it out, though it seems she hasn't realized it yet."

"What?"

Amy thought back to what Tracy might have said or done that would have implicated Rudy. It must have been something he had been present to hear or see. Something he needed to keep covered up, at least for now.

"Where are you going?" she asked, stalling for time.

"Have you ever heard of a small Balkan country called Montenegro?" he asked her.

She thought for a moment, and then she nodded. "Yes. I don't know anything about it though."

"Montenegro doesn't have an extradition treaty with the United States. What you and your sister or anybody else has to say won't matter in the least in a few hours. I've provided for myself quite well for the rest of my hopefully long life, and all I need to do now is get to where I can enjoy it. My plane will land early in the morning. By then, I imagine someone will have found you. Unharmed, I assure you."

"After what happened to Tracy, don't you think this is one of the first places they'll look if I don't come home?"

"They might," he said. "But I'm not leaving you here. I am leaving your phone here, though, in case they want to trace that. Go ahead and put it on the floor." He shook his head when she hesitated. "Don't force me."

He still had one hand in his pocket. She pulled her phone out of her purse and put it on the floor.

"Now what?"

He nodded toward the chair. "Now I make sure you're easy to handle. Go on."

Amy thought again about what he might be up to. Apparently, he'd accumulated a large amount of money and stashed it somewhere out of the country. Money he had promised to Eve and Lyle and small investors like Carol Tomlinson, who'd taken what little they had and given it to him to invest for them.

"You stole Carol's jewelry and coin collection, didn't you? Besides the money you took from her, you took the few valuables she had too."

"She has a habit of telling everything about herself," Rudy said indifferently. "It wasn't hard to get her to tell me what she had and where she kept it and when she would be out."

"You don't care who you lie to, do you? Is that how you got Eve to lie for you and Lyle to steal for you? They were both desperate for money, and you promised it to them. Now neither of them will get anything."

"No, they won't."

"All Lyle knew is that you needed that yearbook," she continued. "He didn't care why. You told him you were going to keep him from losing the boat. And you told Eve you would help her with her son's

225

trust fund. All they had to do was stand by you. But now you're leaving them both high and dry."

He laughed almost soundlessly. It seemed like everybody aboard the *Lucky Chance* had something to hide. *But where does Rudy fit in? What do autographs from decades ago have to do with his fraudulent schemes?* She shook her head. She didn't have time to worry about that now. She had to get herself out of this mess she'd walked into.

She tried to swallow, but her throat was too dry. "Where are you going to take me?"

"Don't worry about that. You'll be safe and reasonably comfortable. When I've reached my new home, I'll make sure to notify the authorities where they can find you, just in case you haven't been found by then. Now, come sit down."

He bent over to pick up the tape, and she could tell his jacket pocket didn't hang the right way, not if it had something heavy, some kind of weapon in it. Was the whole hand in the pocket thing just a charade?

She clutched her purse in both hands and ran toward the chair, breathing a desperate prayer for courage. For help.

Before he could straighten up, she swung the purse and hit him on the head, knocking him to the floor. The corner of the chair back caught him squarely in the temple as he fell, and to her surprise, the hair on top of his head flew off and landed on the floor.

"A toupee," she breathed, but she didn't have time to wonder about that.

She grabbed the roll of tape he had dropped, pulled his arms behind his back, and strapped his wrists together.

"Wha—" he muttered, unable to put up any real resistance as he came to. "You can't—"

"I can," she said, her pulse racing, "and I just did." She took him by one arm and helped him up enough so he could collapse into the chair. "Don't get up."

Before he could steady himself, she strapped his ankles to the front legs of the chair and then, to be extra sure, taped his wrists to one of the slats in the chair back. Then she wiped the film of sweat from her upper lip. She couldn't remember being so scared in her whole life.

She picked up her phone from the floor and called Dale. He answered immediately.

"Amy. What can I do for you?"

"You can come out to Robert West's boathouse and pick up a thief and swindler I think you'll be interested in."

"Oh, really? Anybody I know?"

"He goes by the name of Rudy Daheim."

"Rudy?" Dale asked. "The theater guy? What's that about?"

"It's a long story. You'd better come out right away, and I'll tell you all about it."

"On my way. Are you okay there?"

"I think so, but the sooner you get here, the better I'll feel."

"I'm coming," he said, and ended the call.

Amy wished she could call Miles, but his phone was most likely in one of Rudy's pockets. Tracy was probably not home from Wayland yet. She thought about calling Olivia and checking on the kids, but she didn't want to worry them. Before she could consider what else she should do, her phone rang. Relief surged through her when she saw who it was.

"Tracy. Am I glad to hear from you."

"Are you all right?" Tracy said. "You sound like you just ran a mile."

"I'm all right now," Amy said. "It's been a little touch-and-go here. Are you on your way home?"

"Jeff and I are just getting into Canton. Are you sure everything's okay?"

"I ran into a little bit of trouble at Robert's boathouse."

"The boathouse?" Tracy asked. "What in the world are you doing there?"

"I promise everything is okay, and Dale is on his way out. Can you and Jeff come too?"

"What's going on?" Jeff asked in the background.

"It's Amy," Tracy told him. "She wants us to go to Robert's boathouse. Dale is on his way too."

"Is she all right?" Jeff asked.

"She says so." Tracy spoke into the phone again. "Tell me what's going on, Amy."

"It's a long story. He stole Miles's phone and then texted me, asking me to come over here. I thought it was Miles. He said he had found something that would solve the case."

"He?" Tracy asked. "Who's he?"

"It's Rudy. He's been stealing from his investors and stashing the money out of the country. He planned to leave tonight before anybody realized it, but he didn't want us looking at the autographs in your yearbook."

"Why? I mean, yes, it pretty much had to be the autographs," Tracy said. "They're the only thing that makes my book different from Eve's or anybody else's, but why?"

"He said you had almost figured something out and he couldn't let you see those autographs before he was safely out of the country."

"But the yearbook is gone."

"No, it's not. Miles and I went to the *Lucky Chance* to get the screen, and Dale was there searching Lyle's office and cabin for evidence in your kidnapping. He found your yearbook in Lyle's things."

Amy described what had happened while she and Miles were on the showboat.

"You're kidding," Tracy said. "Looks like I picked the wrong time to be out of town."

"I wish you had been here," Amy said. "Things probably wouldn't have gotten so crazy."

"But why would Lyle steal my yearbook? That's crazier than anything else that's happened."

"Rudy was the one who wanted it. I tried to get it for you, but Dale said he had to keep it in evidence. He made copies for me of the pages you needed for your article, and Rudy wanted me to give them to him."

"Okay, I take it back about Lyle being the craziest thing. Why would Rudy want copies of those autographs?"

"He didn't want them. He just didn't want you to see them."

For a moment, only the hum of the car engine and surrounding traffic came from Tracy's end of the line.

"What did I see that had anything to do with the autographs?" she said finally. "Or somebody else's autograph?"

"The only writing of Rudy's you saw was—" Amy caught her breath. "That card he sent Eve with the lavender roses. Remember?"

Rudy glared at her from his chair, clear-eyed again.

"I remember," Tracy said. "Do you think the writing looked like one of the autographs from the book?"

"I can't picture it exactly. I just remember it was kind of spiky."

"Would you describe any of the autographs like that?"

Amy shuffled through the pages. "Maybe Bryan Ulmer's, but he—" She gasped. "Bryan Ulmer."

"He's dead," Tracy reminded her.

Rudy's glare turned hotter and fiercer as Amy approached him.

"Amy?" Tracy pressed.

"Maybe not," Amy said.

She walked around him, comparing him to the boy in the picture. *"Voted most likely to end up rich or in jail. HA!"* It was hard to tell much from a black-and-white photocopy of a thirty-six-year-old yearbook photo, but she stopped behind him, studying his now-uncovered scalp.

He twisted around to scowl at her. "What are you looking at?"

She didn't answer him. She merely examined the old, whitish scar that made an almost perfect U-shape on top of his head.

"Amy?" Tracy said.

"Do you remember what Bryan Ulmer's surgery scar looked like?" Amy asked her. "And where it was exactly?"

"It's been a long time," Tracy said. "If I remember right, it was big, about the size of a horseshoe, on top of his head but kind of to the right. The other guys used to say—"

"It's him."

Chapter Twenty-Two

*J*ust then, Amy heard the police siren outside the boathouse, and relief flooded through her. "Dale's here," she told her sister.

"Good," Tracy said. "Jeff and I just turned onto the little road that leads there. We should be with you in a minute or two. But are you sure? You're sure it's Bryan?"

"It has to be. He's got a scar on his head like you described."

"How can you tell through his hair?" Tracy asked.

Amy couldn't help a low laugh. "He wore a toupee."

"So is he the one behind the kidnapping?" asked Jeff.

"He says he's not," said Amy. "And I don't know why, but I believe him."

"Amy, are you all right?"

Dale stood in the doorway, and Amy went to him.

"Just fine. Hang on a second." She turned back to her phone. "Dale's here, Tracy. I'll see you in a minute."

"We're pulling up now," Tracy said. "Be right in."

Amy ended the call and went over to Dale, who was examining Rudy's electrical-tape restraints.

"Remind me to stay on your good side," he said.

"Let me out of here, Officer," Rudy demanded. "This is ridiculous."

"Okay." Dale cut the tape off Rudy's wrists and replaced it with handcuffs. Then he cut Rudy's ankles free. "Now tell me how we got to this point."

Tracy and Jeff came in while Amy was explaining how Rudy had lured her and how he had intended to keep her confined somewhere until he was safely out of the country.

"He didn't tell me where he was going to take me," she told Dale. "He said he would leave my phone here in case someone tried to track it, but that he was going to take me somewhere else."

Jeff shook his head, equal parts amazement and admiration in his expression. "How did he end up being the one in the chair?"

"Prayer," Amy said. "He leaned over to pick up the roll of tape, and I hit him with my purse. He banged his head on the back of the chair, and that disoriented him long enough for me to tape him to the chair until Dale got here."

"Are you crazy?" Tracy said. She wrapped Amy in a hug. "Your guardian angel must have been working overtime."

Rudy pursed his lips. "I have never been a violent person, and I assured your sister that I had no intention of harming her."

Tracy stepped back from Amy and looked him over. "Bryan. I almost can't believe it's you, after all this time."

"You knew him before now?" Dale asked, getting out his notebook and pen.

"We went to high school together. He signed my yearbook."

"Ah," Dale said. "So that's where the yearbook comes in."

"Right," Amy said. "He knew Tracy had seen his writing on the card for Eve's roses and it was only a matter of time before she made the connection to Bryan Ulmer's autograph in her yearbook."

"Just a couple more hours," Rudy muttered. "I would have been clear of all this."

"You've been saying you think you've seen him before, Tracy," Amy said. "Now you know why."

"And we thought he looked too young to be sixty-five," Tracy said. "I knew that didn't seem right to me."

"It's the only thing that makes sense," Amy said. "He must have disappeared on 9/11 to get out of the fraud charges he was facing back then."

"What an opportunist," Tracy said tightly. "And tomorrow's the anniversary of the attack. He used that tragedy to get out of responsibility for defrauding who knows how many people and to go on to defraud who knows how many more."

"Yes, he's an impressive opportunist." Amy looked into the cold fury in Rudy's eyes. "You'd be amazed, Tracy, at how quick he was to figure out a way to get me out here. I almost feel sorry for Eve, and even Lyle. Seems like he's pretty good at manipulating people, even people who are clearly pretty good at fraud themselves."

"You can't prove anything," Rudy growled.

"I can prove you stole Miles's phone and lured me out here to kidnap me," Amy said coolly. "That's a start."

"You know he has the phone?" Dale asked, looking Rudy over.

"I know he texted me from the phone," Amy said. "I'm almost positive he has it on him."

Dale patted him down and took a phone out of his jacket pocket. So that was what he'd been trying to intimidate her with.

"Is this the one?" Dale asked.

Amy nodded. "I'm sure it is. If you turn it on, you'll see the wallpaper is a picture of a little boy and girl, both of them with dark hair and eyes. Or I can call Miles's number from my phone. I'm sure it will ring."

Dale had already turned on the phone, and there, as expected, was the picture of Colton and Natalie. "Good enough for me," he said, and he put Miles's phone into an evidence bag. Then he did the same with the hairpiece on the floor. "I guess this is evidence too."

Rudy gave him a sour look and then winced. His right temple was turning a deep purple. The corner of the chair back hadn't done him any good.

"We haven't had cause to search his hotel room yet," Dale said, "but I don't think the judge will have any trouble issuing a warrant based on what we have now. Want to tell us what we'll find, Mr. Daheim?"

Rudy pressed his lips together and said nothing.

"Tell me one thing," Amy said, bending down a little to have her eyes even with his. "Carol's jewelry and her husband's coin collection mean a lot to her. Much more than their monetary value. Do you still have them?"

He merely glared at her.

"She never did anything to hurt you," she said. "You can't get any use out of those things now. Tell us where they are. I'll ask them to consider that at your trial."

He snorted. "That'll make a huge difference."

"It won't hurt," she said, letting a touch of pleading into her voice. "Carol liked you so much. I can't believe you didn't like her. At least a little."

Rudy rolled his eyes and then exhaled heavily. "Okay. My carry-on is in my hotel room. The coins and jewelry are in it. I was supposed to meet a buyer on my way to the airport."

"It'll be evidence," Dale told him. "But we can tell Mrs. Tomlinson we've recovered it. I'm sure that'll make her feel much better."

"Thank you," Amy said.

"I told you all along I'd end up rich or in jail. Looks like I did both." He shrugged. "I've been scamming people most of my life. It had to end sometime."

Just then, Amy's phone rang again, and she saw it was Olivia, probably wondering where she was.

"Olivia. I'm sorry. I ended up in a little situation. I'm—"

"Amy, it's me."

She gasped. "Miles. Oh, I'm so glad to hear your voice. I wanted to call you right away, but I know you don't have your phone."

"How do you know? After I finished with my patient, I returned to the *Lucky Chance* to look for it, but I couldn't find it. So I came to your house, and Olivia said you'd suddenly had to go somewhere."

"Your phone is here. At Robert West's boathouse."

"What in the world are you doing there?" Miles asked.

"It's a very long story. Can you wait there with the kids until I can get home?" She looked questioningly at Dale. "It shouldn't be too much longer, right?"

He gave her a nod, and she turned back to the phone.

"Miles? Do you mind paying Olivia? I'll settle with you when I get there."

"Don't be silly," Miles said. "I'll take care of it. She's watching my kids too."

"Thanks. I'll be home soon."

"Are you sure you're all right?" he asked.

"It's been…interesting. But, yes, I'm fine, and we finally know what's been going on all this time. I'll be there in a little while."

"Okay. Drive carefully. Bring my phone."

"Uh, that might be a problem. Hold on." She looked at Dale. "I guess the phone is evidence now?"

"I'm afraid so," Dale said. "We'll try to get it back to Miles as soon as possible."

"I'll tell him." Amy turned to her phone again. "Dale says you'll have to wait a while, but he'll return your phone as soon as possible."

"I guess I can get a temporary one," Miles said.

"I'd better get going now. See you soon."

"Okay, honey," he said, his voice taking on a sudden tenderness. "Take care of yourself."

"I will." She hung up, feeling a little self-conscious with everybody looking at her. "Miles is with the kids. I should probably get home as soon as I can. What else do you need from me, Dale?"

"I've got what I need for right now. I'll need you and Miles to come make formal statements about Mr. Daheim." Dale pulled Rudy to his feet. "This guy and I are going to have a nice long talk."

Rudy looked at Tracy. "I guess you'll have a pretty interesting article to write now."

"It may have to be a series," Tracy said. "A long one."

He gave her a sardonic smile. "I'll give you an exclusive."

"Come on," Dale said, giving his arm a tug. "Amy, would you mind calling Mr. West and telling him what's happened here? After everything is checked out forensically, he'll want to replace the lock."

"I'll call him," Tracy said. "I think Amy's eager to get home."

"I've had easier days," Amy admitted.

Home sounded awfully good to her just then.

"Why don't all of you go?" Dale suggested. "I'll put the suspect in my car and then put up some crime-scene tape and wait until somebody gets here to examine the scene."

"Thanks, Dale," Amy said. "I was really glad to see you when you got here."

He winked. "Best part of the job."

He led Rudy out to the squad car. Amy followed Jeff and Tracy out to their car.

"Do you want us to take you home?" Tracy asked her. "We can bring you back to pick up your car later."

"No, that's okay," Amy said. "I'd rather drive myself. And, really, I'm okay. It could have been much worse."

"Yeah," Tracy said. "Bryan always was a weasel, but I don't remember him ever getting rough with anybody."

"Don't forget to call Robert," Amy said. "I still don't understand what was going on with Eve and Fran hearing him and Lyle arguing when he couldn't possibly have been there."

"I think Eve and Fran have a lot more serious things to deal with," Tracy said, "but maybe we'll find out eventually. If Lyle ever decides to admit what was going on in the first place. Hard to believe getting kidnapped didn't have anything to do with what Rudy was up to."

"He and Lyle have both been arrested," Jeff said, "so maybe I don't have to worry about either of you anymore...until the next time you get into trouble."

Tracy chuckled and playfully punched his arm.

"I'll talk to both of you later," Amy said. "Right now, I'm going home."

"Call me later," Tracy said as she got into her car.

"I will."

Amy waved and got into her own car. She nodded at Dale, who was talking on his radio, and then she looked at Rudy one last time. He coolly met her gaze. He'd spent decades successfully defrauding people. It was amazing it had taken this long to catch him.

"About time," she murmured, and then, with a sigh of relief, she headed for home.

All four kids ran to her when she got back to the house, all clamoring to tell her what they'd been doing and asking where she'd been.

"I had some business to take care of," she told them. "But I'm all done for today."

Miles wrapped her in a hug and gave her a quick kiss. "Everything all right?"

"Just tired," she said. "Everything okay here?"

"We're doing fine. They're still working on building that castle, but Olivia went home a while ago."

"Come see," Jana said, taking Amy by the hand, and they all went to the guest room.

The castle still needed a lot of work, but they'd gotten quite a ways on it.

"It's going to take a while to get that done," Miles said with a glance at Amy, "so you kids better get to work again."

"Matt finished the drawbridge, and I put this tower together," Colton told her, showing Amy his handiwork. "Do you like it?"

Amy smiled at him. "You did a great job."

He gave her a shy smile in return, and then Matt called him over to help find a particular piece he was looking for.

Miles slipped an arm around her, and they watched the kids play.

"They have a great time together," he said.

She leaned against him. "I'm glad they're friends."

"I'm glad we're friends," he murmured, nuzzling her hair. "And more than friends."

She smiled into his eyes. "Me too."

"You look worn out. Why don't we go sit down and you can tell me all about what happened."

"I'd like that." She turned to the kids again. "We'll be in the kitchen. Play nice."

"Okay, Mom," Jana said, looking up from the Legos she was putting together. "You and Dr. Miles play nice too."

Amy laughed. "We will."

Miles took her hand as they walked to the kitchen and then pulled out a chair for her at the table.

"I'll make some coffee. You just relax."

"That'd be nice," she said.

While he worked, she told him what had happened with Rudy at the boathouse.

"I'm sorry I wasn't with you," Miles said when she was done.

"If you'd been with me, he never would have gotten me out to the boathouse in the first place."

"I guess not." He brought two cups of delicious-smelling coffee to the table and sat down next to her. "I don't like being without my phone though."

"It won't be for long, I hope. Dale said they would get it to you as soon as possible."

"The most important thing is that you're safe." Miles tucked a strand of her hair behind her ear. "Now I know how Jeff must have felt when he found out after the fact that Tracy was in trouble."

"This wasn't nearly as scary as what happened to her, but I'm glad it's over and we can get back to what we were doing last night."

"You mean this?" he asked, and he leaned over and gave her a soft kiss.

"Yes," she admitted, feeling a touch of warmth come into her cheeks. "And talking about where we go from here."

"For now, on a lot of dates." He gave her another kiss. "And then we see. I've been wanting to ask you out for a long time."

"I've been wanting that too, but we did already have our first date."

"Thanks to Tracy and the kids." He laughed and pulled her into his arms. "We'd better watch out. Who knows what kind of trouble our little gang will get us into."

Chapter Twenty-Three

*A*my and Tracy met for coffee after school the next day at the River Queen Café while Jana and Matt played at Natalie and Colton's house. Amy had brought the copies of Tracy's yearbook pages for her to look at.

"I knew there was something odd about Rudy's writing," Tracy said. "Or should I say Bryan's?"

"He nearly got away with it." Amy shook her head. "Remember what Dad used to say? He's the type who'd climb a tree and tell a lie when he could have stood on the ground and told the truth."

Tracy chuckled. "I remember that. After this, it looks like Rudy's not going to be handling anybody's money anytime soon. But I still don't understand why—"

She broke off when her phone rang.

"Hey, it's Dale," she said, and she tapped the icon to answer. "Hi, Dale." She paused a moment, listening. "That's great. I'm with Amy. Okay. Yeah." She listened again and then started slowly shaking her head. "Wow. You're kidding me. Okay. Thanks for letting us know. Talk to you later."

She hung up, still shaking her head.

"What did he say?" Amy asked. "Is it about Rudy?"

"Looks like Fran really was blackmailing Eve. Eve filed a complaint against her for sending those statements to Flynn. Now they're both in trouble."

"Wow is right."

"And Lyle claims that Fran was also blackmailing him," Tracy said. "She tried to claim that the money they had been giving her was just a gift and that they're blowing her little bit of snooping out of proportion, but Dale's not buying that. Not with Eve's and Lyle's testimony against her. What a tangled web it all is. Poor Eve. I really hope she can work things out with her son."

"Me too. And I feel bad for all the people who are going to be out of jobs because the showboat has to shut down."

"Yeah." Tracy sighed. "But Rudy was never going to give Lyle any money, so it was going to happen anyway." She paused. "Maybe some investor will take over the whole thing, boat, plays, and all. I think I'll make that suggestion when I write my article about all this. Danny and everybody on the boat could end up better off than before."

"I hope so," Amy said. "But they'll have to do it without Lyle. And maybe even without Eve."

"Dale had something else to say about Lyle. Something that answers our last question."

"About why Lyle had you kidnapped?"

"He finally cracked. Dale said that after Lyle found out Rudy planned to leave the country and leave him high and dry on the boat repossession, he spilled everything. He even admitted that he came home from Vegas Saturday night, not Monday like he said. I guess he figures he's losing the *Lucky Chance* and his theatrical company, so he might as well come clean."

"What did he say?" Amy pressed. "Why did he have you kid-napped?"

"To get back at me."

Amy and Tracy turned around to see Robert West standing by their table. With him was a younger man, probably not yet thirty, dressed in jeans and a T-shirt with the name of some rock band printed on it.

"This is my grandson," Robert said. "Lin, this is Tracy Doyle and Amy Allen. I told you about them. They're the ones who've been in the middle of this mess all along."

"Hi," Lin said. "Good to meet you. Grandpa's been worried about you. We're both glad all this is over."

"We are too," Tracy said. "Dale must have called your grandfa-ther before he called me a minute ago."

"He did," Robert said, looking quite pleased with himself. "So you know already, right?"

"Know what?" Amy said. "Will you both please sit down and tell me what Dale said?"

Robert chuckled, and he and Lin took a seat.

"I told you first thing about me and Lyle," Robert said, waving for the waitress to bring two more cups of coffee to the table. "I told him I was going to make sure he didn't get away with what he'd done to the captain all those years ago, so he wanted me to have trouble enough myself that I didn't have time to trouble him. He dumped you in my boathouse to make me look guilty."

"We thought that might be the case a while ago," Amy said, "but it seemed like a pretty lame reason for kidnapping someone."

"Oh, getting me into trouble was just a side benefit," Robert said. "Those men were actually supposed to kidnap that book-keeper, Fran. Lyle confessed that she'd been blackmailing him, and he wanted to put a good scare into her so she'd stop. When Lyle saw that they got you instead, Tracy, he ended the whole thing. He thought he was going to get money from Rudy, so he wasn't worried about Fran after that anyway. Didn't quite work out the way he planned."

"We wondered if it could be Lyle, because he was the only one we could think of from the boat who might not have known that Tracy took Fran's place," Amy said. "Even though he came back on Saturday night, he must have laid low and not heard about the Sunday night performance."

"So Fran and Eve lied when they said they heard you and Lyle arguing that morning before he left town," Tracy said.

Robert glanced at his grandson. "Actually, no."

"But you weren't there," Amy protested. "You said you were driving to Springfield and back that morning."

"He was," Lin said. "I was the one arguing with Lyle that morning."

Amy and Tracy looked at each other and then back at him.

"But Fran and Eve both heard Lyle arguing with somebody he called Robert," Amy said. "You're not—"

"He is," Robert said. "His middle name is Robert. The family calls him Lin, but otherwise he prefers Robert."

Lin grimaced. "If you knew how many times I was teased in school for having a girl's name..."

"It's a fine old family name," Robert said, a twinkle in his eye.

"Anyway," Lin said, "I knew how much trouble Lyle was giving Grandpa, and I went to talk to him about it. We didn't come to blows, but nearly. I would have told the police about it, but nobody mentioned it to me until today. I was out camping with friends until late yesterday, and Grandpa and I didn't talk about the case until Dale called him a little while ago. I'm glad you two were here so we could straighten things out."

"It wasn't just by chance," Robert admitted with a wink at Tracy. "We went by your house, and your husband told us where you and Amy were."

"I'm happy you did," Tracy said.

"I am too," Amy added. "It's nice to finally know where all the pieces fit."

They chatted a while longer about the case, and then Robert and Lin left the café.

"I'm glad Robert didn't actually do anything wrong," Amy said.

"Looks like he's about the only one involved in this case who didn't," Tracy said.

"He's a good man. There aren't too many of them around these days."

"Oh, I wouldn't say so." Tracy gave Amy a smug little glance. "Seems like you ended up with an awfully good one yourself."

"We'll see about that," Amy said, but she couldn't keep a smile from crossing her face when she thought about going to pick up the kids at Miles's house in a little while. "We'll see."

Dear Reader,

I was so excited when my wonderful editors said it was time for Miles and Amy to finally start dating. Amy's been on her own for a long time now, and has for many years regretted breaking up with Miles after they finished school. She thought she wanted more than what he and little Canton could offer her, and when she realized she was wrong, she was sure she had forever missed her chance.

Once she and Miles admitted how they really felt about each other, she found out that, truly, "the best is yet to be." It was fun getting them together, albeit with a little outside help, and I'm looking forward to seeing their relationship grow and strengthen over the rest of the series as they blend their two families into one.

It's never too late for a second chance.

Blessings!
DeAnna

About The Author

*D*eAnna Julie Dodson has always been an avid reader and a lover of storytelling, whether on the page, the screen, or the stage. This, along with her keen interest in history and her Christian faith, shows in her many published books about love, forgiveness, and triumph over adversity. A fifth-generation Texan, she makes her home north of Dallas with three spoiled cats and, when not writing, spends her free time quilting, cross-stitching, and watching NHL hockey.

COLLECTIBLES *From* GRANDMA'S ATTIC

Mother of Pearl

*T*he screen that Amy and Tracy loaned Eve for the play aboard the showboat, the *Lucky Chance*, was made of dark lacquered wood and inset with mother-of-pearl. For centuries, artisans from all over the world have used gleaming mother-of-pearl for everything from furniture and other decorative items to jewelry, buttons, watch dials, keys on musical instruments, and even, for the style-conscious quick-draw artist, gun handles. The famously flashy costumes of the Pearly Kings and Queens of London are covered with hundreds, even thousands, of buttons made of mother-of-pearl.

So where does mother-of-pearl come from? Mother-of-pearl is a common name for nacre, the minerals secreted by mollusks that coat the inside of their shells and, in the presence of an irritant, eventually form actual pearls. It is usually cream, white, or off-white, but can come in a variety of colors: gray, silver, yellow, black, blue-green, purple, and even red, depending on the type of mollusk it came from. Most varieties have an iridescent appearance reminiscent of the shifting shimmer of the sea as the light glances off it.

Pearls are generally either strung or set into jewelry pieces and can be extremely valuable. Mother-of-pearl, however, while having the same creamy sheen as the pearl itself, is very thin and is typically applied or inlaid onto another surface. It is far less expensive than pearls due to its abundance in nature and is very versatile. Mother-of-pearl jewelry is suitable for casual, office, or evening wear and always adds a touch of classic style. However, as a needleworker and antique lover, one of my favorite possessions is my old canning jar filled to the brim with vintage mother-of-pearl buttons of all shapes and sizes. They're my favorite!

*Read on for a sneak peek of another exciting book
in the Secrets from Grandma's Attic series!*

In Its Time
By Beth Adams

✦━━━━━━━━━━━✦

racy Doyle dropped her purse on the chair by the kitchen table and set the mail on the counter. She flipped through it quickly. Gas bill, electric bill, one of Jeff's history magazines, postcard, junk mail...

Wait. Tracy pulled the postcard out of the pile and gazed at the picture on the front. It showed Big Ben and the Tower of London, with an iconic red double-decker bus parked in front of it. *Greetings from London* was printed across the bottom.

Sadie nudged Tracy's leg with her nose. Tracy reached down and rubbed the goldendoodle's head absently. "We'll go for a walk in a minute," she said, but didn't look up from the postcard.

Who did they know who had traveled to London? Maybe one of Jeff's colleagues? She flipped the postcard over and squinted at the signature at the bottom. *Lillee.* Who was Lillee? Was the postcard misdelivered? She checked the address and saw—

Oh. Well, that explained it. The postcard was addressed to Pearl Allen. Grandma Pearl. She'd lived in this house until she passed away nearly two years ago. Tracy didn't remember any of Grandma's friends by the name of Lillee, but she certainly hadn't known all of Grandma's friends. Whoever Lillee was, she must not know that Grandma was gone. Tracy read the message Lillee had scrawled on the back of the postcard.

> *I've always wanted to see London, and I finally made it. After a full English breakfast, we're headed to see the crown jewels this morning followed by a proper tea this afternoon. Jim always thought he would hate England, but I think he would have loved it. I hope you're doing well. As always, I will never forget you.*
>
> *Lillee*

Tracy read through the message twice and shook her head. Whoever Lillee was, she sounded like she was having a good time. If she was a contemporary of Grandma's, she had to be nearing triple digits. Tracy was glad she'd made it to London and was enjoying herself. But Tracy should let her know about Grandma. Too bad it was a postcard and not a letter, which would have had a return address. Tracy had no idea how to get in touch with Lillee to give her the news. She'd check through Grandma's address book again, but she'd gone through it thoroughly after Grandma passed. She was pretty sure there was no one named Lillee listed there.

Tracy set the postcard down when Sadie nudged her again. "Okay, girl. Are you ready for your walk?"

Sadie recognized that word. She headed toward the door, and Tracy followed a step behind. She grabbed the leash off the hook, clipped it onto Sadie's collar, and they set off. The air was crisp and clean and the sky a beautiful shade of cerulean that set off the golden and burnt-orange leaves perfectly. October was a glorious month in Missouri, with the oppressive heat of the summer washed away by the cool fall breezes.

The little town of Canton looked especially stunning today. The trees, robed in their autumn finery, set off the beauty of the Victorian homes in this historic part of town. Sadie sniffed at trees and lunged at a squirrel or two, and by the time they made it home again, Tracy felt more relaxed and refreshed. As they walked up the driveway, she saw that Jeff's car was now parked in front of the garage. She went inside, let Sadie off the leash, and smiled at her husband, who was pouring himself a glass of milk at the counter.

"How was your day?" Tracy hung up the leash, and then she walked over, leaned in, and planted a kiss on his cheek.

"Long," Jeff said. "A lecture in the morning and then office hours in the afternoon. But it was good. How about you?"

"It was fine," Tracy said. "I mostly worked on my column." Tracy worked part-time as a reporter for the *Lewis County Times*, the local newspaper.

"What are you writing about this week?"

"The old train depot," Tracy said. She wrote a weekly column where she featured some odd or forgotten piece of local history, and this week she'd decided to focus on the train station on the east side of town. The old brick building was abandoned now, as the trains hadn't stopped at the small towns up and down the Mississippi in many years, but the building had been important to the town once. The railroad coming through had changed Canton from a sleepy river town into a bustling commercial center. Most of the old homes and brick buildings downtown were built once the railroad money had started coming in.

"Nice," Jeff said. "Have you been able to get inside? I bet it would be fascinating to poke around in there."

Jeff was a history professor at the local college, and Tracy loved that he was as passionate about local history as she was.

"I got to go in with Nick yesterday to take pictures. It's pretty beat-up in there. The plaster is crumbling, there's water damage to all the wood, and vandals have broken in over the years, so there's a lot of graffiti. But you can tell it was beautiful once."

"I'd really like to see it," Jeff said. "It's such an important piece of the town's history. It's sad that now it just sits there rotting."

"Maybe someday the town will get together to fix it up," Tracy said. She'd heard of some towns that had transformed their old train stations into museums and restaurants and all kinds of other things. She knew it would be a monumental task, but it might happen someday.

"Let's hope." Jeff turned his attention to the magazine on the counter. "Oh, cool. This one has an article about that ancient Pueblo city they've unearthed in New Mexico."

Tracy had only vaguely heard of it, but she nodded anyway. Jeff moved the magazine and saw the postcard. He picked it up. "Who went to London?"

"One of Grandma's friends," Tracy said. "I was trying to figure out how to track her down to let her know about Grandma."

"That's a good idea." He flipped the postcard over and read the note. "Though I have no idea how you'll be able to find her."

"Find who?"

Tracy looked up and saw her sister, Amy, step into the kitchen, followed by her two children.

"Hi," Tracy said. "You made it."

"Hello," seven-year-old Jana said.

"Hey, Aunt Tracy. Uncle Jeff." Matt nodded at them before making a beeline for Sadie, who gladly looked up from her water dish to roll onto her back so the kids could rub her belly.

"Thank you for watching them tonight," Amy said. Tracy could see Amy had added waves to her hair and put on eye makeup and a hint of lipstick.

"Of course. Have fun." Miles and Amy were going out to their favorite Italian place. They'd dated when they were teenagers and had only recently started dating again. Tracy wasn't sure she'd ever seen Amy happier.

"We won't be out late, since it's a school night."

"Stay out as long as you want. If the kids get tired, they can sleep here until you get back."

"Thanks." Amy pointed to the postcard. "Who are you trying to find?"

"A friend of Grandma's," Tracy said. She handed the postcard to Amy, who looked it over and squinted at it. "We want to let her know that Grandma died, but we don't know how to get in touch with her."

"Lillee," Amy said. "I've seen this before."

"How have you seen this postcard?" Jeff asked. "It just came today."

"No, not this one, specifically." Amy shook her head. "But others from this same person. Grandma has gotten other postcards from her."

"How do you know that?" Tracy asked.

Amy shrugged. "They're up in the attic. Grandma had a whole collection of postcards people sent her over the years up there. I found them a few years ago when I was looking for a program from one of my old dance recitals."

"Why were you looking for a program from a dance recital?" Tracy asked.

"It's a long story. Doesn't matter." Amy shook her head again. "The point is, I found this box of old postcards. Grandma got some from friends who traveled to pretty cool places. Anyway, there were several from someone named Lillee. I remember because it's such a distinctive spelling."

"Are they still up there, do you think?" Jeff asked.

"Unless someone moved them. I can't imagine where else they would be."

Tracy looked at Jeff. "I wonder if there's any contact information for Lillee on any of the other postcards."

"It's probably worth checking out," he said.

"Well, you two have fun with that. The box used to be over by the bookshelves, but who knows where it is now. Anyway, I need to get going." Amy waved as she headed toward the door. "And you two be good," she called to the kids.

"We will," Matt called, still rubbing the belly of a very satisfied Sadie.

"We will," Jana echoed.

As soon as Amy was out the door, Jeff clapped his hands. "We're making pizza for dinner. Who likes pizza?"

"Me!" Jana jumped up, her hand raised in the air. "Can I put the cheese on?"

"Sure." Jeff laughed. "How about I work with these guys to get the pizzas ready while you go up and look for those postcards?" he said to Tracy.

"How did you know that was what I was hoping to do?"

"I've known you for a few years now." The corners of Jeff's eyes crinkled as he smiled at her. "Go on up and see what you can find."

"Thanks. I'll be back soon." Tracy used the rear stairs, the ones they'd discovered during a renovation last year that went directly from the pantry to the attic. She climbed carefully up the narrow steps and stepped out into the unfinished attic. She pulled the string attached to the single bare bulb and blinked as the space filled with light.

Tracy took in a deep breath. She loved the attic smell—a particular blend of must, old paper, and lemon wood polish that always made her think of all the possibilities in the antiques up here. Trunks full of old clothes were shoved against the wall. Heavy pieces of furniture, some covered by sheets, were scattered throughout the space, and boxes containing who knew what were piled everywhere. She made her way carefully over to the bookshelves on the street side of the attic, to the left of the big stained-glass window. The upper shelves were packed with an odd assortment of books—some antique leather-bound volumes and some paperbacks and bestsellers various family members had collected over the years. The lower shelves were filled with more boxes containing papers in unorganized piles. Someday Tracy would have time to go through all of this and sort things out, but today was not that day.

She crouched down and looked at the boxes set on the shelves. MEDICAL PAPERS, one was labeled. BILLS, said another. And there was... ah. There, on the bottom shelf, was a file box labeled POST-CARDS. She pulled it out and carefully lifted it up. She set it on a nearby desk and lifted off the lid. It was filled with postcards, all standing upright. Tracy took out the first one. It had a black-and-white photo of Detroit, Michigan, on the front. She flipped it over and saw that it was addressed to Pearl Allen and was sent to this house. Grandma had grown up in this house, so that made sense.

A message was written in childish handwriting:

> Dear Pearl,
> I hope you're enjoying the summer. We came to Detroit to see my grandparents. I miss home. See you when school starts.
> From,
> Bess

Tracy looked at the upper right-hand corner, where a three-cent stamp was affixed. The postmark indicated that it was sent from Detroit on July 19, 1932. Grandma would have been ten. Bess must have been one of her childhood friends. Grandma had kept this postcard from when she was just a preteen. But then, she wasn't surprised. Grandma had always treasured things that held sentimental value. She set the postcard back in the box and found a few others from Grandma's younger days—notes sent from friends who had visited Niagara Falls, Louisville, Kentucky, and Portland, Maine—and some from high school as well. The postcards went through the decades, into the 1950s and 1960s, all the way up through the later years of Grandma's life. Tracy couldn't be sure, of course, but it seemed like Grandma must have kept every postcard she'd ever received.

Tracy pulled several out at random and set them on the desk. It was fascinating to see how the postcard designs had changed throughout the years, from the black-and-white photos of the 1930s and '40s to the psychedelic illustrations of the '60s to the photos of people in bell-bottoms and with big hair as the decades went on. The fonts and colors changed, and the photos got clearer and more true-to-life and more recognizably contemporary. She could see the evolution of design throughout the decades just in this small little window.

And the messages scrawled on the backs of the postcards were also fascinating. Tracy recognized a few of the senders' names, including Grandma's good friend Eloise, Aunt Abigail, and Tracy's own parents, but most were from people Tracy had never heard of. Some of the postcards were from far-flung destinations, such as Rome and Hong Kong, but the majority were from places closer to home, like Wisconsin and Texas and Florida. Some of the senders had written lengthy descriptions of what they were doing on their trips while others sent short messages—*wish you were here, enjoying our vacation,* or *see you soon.* All of them had taken the time to send postcards to Grandma to let her know they were thinking of her. Tracy imagined Grandma reading each one, smiling. She had clearly loved getting them to have saved so many throughout the years.

It would take forever to read all of these, but it would be fascinating. Tracy wished she could just sit there and dig into them, but she needed to get downstairs and help Jeff with the kids. She slipped the postcards back into the box. She would look through them more carefully later and see if she could find the ones sent by Lillee that Amy had mentioned. If there were any clues to help her figure out how to get ahold of Lillee, Tracy would find them.

Tracy and Jeff ate pizza with the kids, and they were halfway through *The Muppet Movie* when Amy showed up to take them home. After the kids and Amy left, Jeff went upstairs to get ready for bed and Tracy sat down at the table, thinking she would look through a few dozen postcards to try to find the ones from Lillee. She would just check the signatures, she decided, and that would allow her to move through them quickly. She started at the back, with the most recent postcards, and an hour later, she was halfway through the box. Try as she might, she couldn't stop herself from looking at more than the signature. She wanted to know when they were sent, where they were sent from, and what each person had to say. And then she had to turn them over to see what was featured on each. A picture of racks of cowboy boots had come from Dallas, a white-sand beach from Anna Maria Island in Florida, and a sailboat on a huge lake was from Michigan. The postcard said almost as much about the person who chose it as it did about the place, Tracy decided.

"Are you coming to bed?" Jeff came down the stairs, rubbing his eyes. He walked over to the cabinet, pulled out a glass, and got himself a drink of water.

"Yes," Tracy said, pushing herself up. "Sorry. I got distracted."

"The postcards will still be there in the morning," Jeff said. "If Lillee doesn't know about Grandma by now, waiting a few more hours isn't going to hurt her."

Tracy set the cards she'd examined in a stack and reluctantly followed him up to bed.

When the alarm went off what seemed like just a few minutes later, Tracy rolled over and groaned. Surely it couldn't be morning already. But she saw that Jeff was gone, no doubt on his morning run, and she could smell the scent of coffee wafting up the stairs. He'd already brewed a pot. God bless that man. She silenced the alarm, pushed herself up, and glanced at her phone. She blinked when she saw a text from her boss. It had come in a half hour ago. What was he doing texting her so early? GET DOWN TO THE RIVER AS SOON AS YOU CAN, he'd written. THERE'S SOMETHING BIG YOU NEED TO SEE.